A Garden, a Pig and Me

A Year at Torryburn

Jenny Ferguson

Hardie Grant Books

First published in 1999
by Hardie Grant Books
Level 3, 44 Caroline Street
South Yarra Victoria 3141

National Library of Australia Cataloguing-in-Publication Data:
Ferguson, Jenny, 1947-

ISBN 1 86498 048 6

1. Ferguson, Jenny, 1947- -Diaries. 2. Cookery – New South Wales – Hunter
Valley. 3. Gardens – New South Wales – Hunter Valley. I. Title.

635.099442

Cover and text design by Phil Campbell
Photography by Rodney Weidland, Andre Wohler, Jackie Wisbey and
    Jenny Ferguson
Food styling by Stephen Troy
Garden maps drawn by Amanda Grainger
Produced by Tien Wah Press
Printed and bound in Singapore

In memory of my mother, Joan Jarvis

LIFE BEGINS WHEN YOU START A GARDEN
CHINESE PROVERB

For Nicks mum,

with good wishes

Jenny Ferguson

Contents

A Year at Torryburn: garden notes and food   24

Introduction

I WROTE what follows for myself. I wanted to record a year in the garden in order to remember all that went on there. Just the little things, like the flowers, the weather, the animals, our successes and failures alike, and also to understand my own feelings – my passion for this undertaking while it was still at its height, before it all changed and I turned to something else.

That has been the story of my life, becoming obsessed, taking that obsession to some sort of limit in order to understand it, feel confident and comfortable with it, then moving on.

Sometimes the hard bit is discovering what the passion is, if indeed one exists at all. Such things do not always leap out with fanfare and flashing lights all clear and recognisable, but rather sneak up gradually, surprising you as much as anyone else. The next difficulty is knowing what to do about it, and then being prepared to take risks and even appear crazy in the attempt to turn yearnings into reality.

Opening a restaurant in 1978 after years of tedious teaching was, for me, a truly frightening leap into the dark. But I had a passion for cooking that could not be contained in any conventional way. Some people at the time did think I was crazy and said so, but following my own inclination against the opinion of doomsayers meant that I would never again be afraid of doing anything that I had an inner longing for.

I think that that is how this garden in rural New South Wales, deep in the Paterson Valley north of Newcastle, came about. Without being the slightest bit worried about what other people might think – or even the fact that I didn't really know what I was doing – I did what I wanted and learnt as I went along.

Food is an important part of the whole. I cannot pretend that cooking is now nothing to me and gardening is everything, because that is not true. Cooking is still an important part of the pleasure of each day, but not intense like it used to be and much more enjoyable. I rarely follow recipes and those recorded here are not always spelt out in precise detail.

What remains are thoughts. Gardening is the perfect occupation for thinking, not only about What's for dinner?, or Do the buddleias need cutting back yet?, but the really big questions too like, Why am I here? and What am I to do?

This book is a very personal account of a year in a garden. It is the year after my Mother died and I felt my world would never be the same again. It is, in one way, an internal view of the external life, as much about feelings as gardening or food. It is not a practical manual, although there is a lot of practical advice given. It is, I think, more about struggling to find meaning, to be inspired or optimistic, in tune with nature, nurturing and creating beauty, in order to find peace and a purpose in life.

Writing about a year in my life has helped to make this passing of time achieve a sense of shape and meaning. However trivial and homely our lives, there is something to be made of them. That is what I have tried to do here – to make something of mine.

Acknowledgments

FIRST and foremost, a special thank you to my husband Rob, who continues, after thirty-something years, to have enough faith in me and my schemes to go on giving his encouragement and support in whatever I do, graciously and even enthusiastically. He believes in people following their dreams and he has certainly helped me to follow mine.

Thank you, also, to all who have helped over the years in the garden. In particular, in the early days, Liz Maines and Gail Boxell, and as I write, David Cox, James Baker and Amanda Grainger. A warm thank you to Amanda for drawing the beautiful garden maps used in this book, for horticultural help, and for her enthusiasm in the ongoing design and planting with the garden.

Thank you to my brother Mark Jarvis for reading recipes, talking food and giving advice culinary and otherwise so generously. Special thanks to photographer extraordinaire, Rodney Weidland, for turning up on my doorstep once more with camera at the ready and for introducing me to Andre Vorhler and Jackie Wisbey who worked in the broiling sun to produce their superb photographs as well. Thanks too, to Stephen Troy for his special flair arranging food, flowers and other objects and for his friendship and encouragement in this sometimes lonely part of the world.

Finally it is my mother to whom I bid thanks – for teaching me, with her own special quiet wisdom, about life and how to live it, and for instilling a love of all things creative. Whether cooking or gardening, writing or painting, she always managed to rise above the daily tedium by having a project of some kind on the go - half a dozen paintings she was working on, a novel half completed, written in the small hours of yet another sleepless morning, a new recipe for a pudding she thought we all might like. Hers was an unsung, and for the most part, unpraised ability to do many things very well. Her great gift was to encourage others to do likewise.

Making a Garden

Torryburn

THE DOROTHEA MACKELLAR CONNECTION

THE CREEK that dog-legs its way across the width of the property is the McIntyre, named after John McIntyre who was the first pioneer to live here, in 1821. The remnants of the house built at this time can be seen in the garden: a tumbledown brick fireplace which is all that remains of the old kitchen, and the restored stone laundry, one of the two rooms that comprised the rest of the house, built by convicts.

All sorts of stories surround John McIntyre and his cruelty towards the convicts. In the end, he disappeared, thought murdered, though his body was never found. In December 1832 four convicts were convicted for his murder and sentenced to be hanged, but someone else confessed in time, the convicts were pardoned, and the trial seen for the sham that it was.

In 1881 the house that stands today was built. The property of 4000 acres was considered a model of farm management at the time. Over the years Torryburn has been home to a variety of owners, but none more famous than the young lady of thirteen who came to live here with her family in 1898.

Charles Mackellar purchased the property at the beginning of a severe drought. This event must have made a lasting impression on the young Dorothea. Her well-loved poem 'My Country' contains the lines

Over the thirsty paddocks
Watch, after many days
The filmy veil of greenness
That thickens as we gaze.

In 1997 the local historical society in Paterson published a book *The Dorothea Mackellar 'My Country' Paterson Valley Connection* by Val Anderson. It explores the influence that the Torryburn years had on the poem.

Val Anderson wrote: 'Dorothea Mackellar acknowledged the lasting Torryburn inspiration in several interviews, such as one given in 1964 when she said: "There had been a drought, then rain, and we all danced in the flooding rain. I was on the verandah writing a long letter to a friend in England. The paddock was cracked from drought, a dark colour. As I wrote the letter, the land to horizon became green. After the poem was published people wrote to me and said they knew exactly what I meant, but they did not have the words for it, literally."'

The property today is nowhere near the size it was in Dorothea Mackellar's time. When we came to Torryburn, in December 1988, it was an 800-acre farm running beef cattle in combination with Arab horses. As we were not interested in cattle farming we immediately sold a 400-acre parcel of hill country that did not fit our needs, and began to turn what was left into a farm suitable for raising thoroughbred horses.

Making a Start

SETTING up the farm was my job. I'm not sure that I fully knew it at the time, but bit by bit I took on the responsibility of planning and organising the workmen to do it. New stables with exercise yards were built, along with a manager's house and a smaller cottage for farm staff, roads were gravelled, drainage improved, dams dug, new paddocks laid out and fenced, and farm machinery purchased.

At night I took agricultural handbooks to bed. I studied books on ploughing, fertilisers, grasses, horses' dietary needs, soil improvement, water conservation and re-forestation. I called in soil and water experts and agronomists. I visited other studs, taking copious notes, and came at last to understand how I wanted to look after my land.

The principle was simple and will be recognised by any gardener. First and foremost, before anything else, respect and look after the soil.

So I devised a plan that was a combination of resting and feeding. I would rest the soil by rotating livestock, and not overstocking in the first place, and feed it mainly with organic fertilisers, adding humus by mulching, aerating it by judicious ploughing and planting trees to give shelter to livestock and protection from winds to both land and animals. The first success of this plan was a measured increase in topsoil.

But all this was not without its difficulties. Some of the men hired in those days could not comprehend what I was trying to do. Perhaps I should not blame them too much for that. Sometimes I don't quite understand what I'm doing myself and rely on an intuitive blending of seemingly disconnected bits of information – not always easy to put into words. They could not connect with my vision. I think some of them didn't really want to connect.

What I found most hurtful was their reluctance to do what I wanted, when it was, after all, my farm. There seemed to be insurmountable problems of communication, which exhausted me. At times this became open conflict. Through their eyes I was just another woman from the city, ignorant of country ways, and out of place telling men what to do. Through my eyes they were ignorant, stuck in the past and unforgivably chauvinistic.

In those early days there was so much to sort out and do, and I needed a good team to help me do it. Now, almost ten years later, Torryburn whirs along happily like a well-oiled machine, and if the men who work here think me difficult or even demented, they are too polite to say so! The important thing is to listen and go on learning. For the most part we are in tune with each other, the vision is on track, and we are all beavering away in the same direction.

The House

THE 1881 house was designed by J.W. Pendor, of Maitland. He was an important architect in his day, and Pendor Place in Maitland is named after him.

The style was classic Victorian Italianate. Despite years of neglect – the verandah netted in with chicken wire, holes in the windows plugged with newspaper, an outdoor toilet filled with thick dusty webs and large hairy spiders – we could see when we inspected it that Torryburn had once been a house of great elegance.

However, the wrought-iron lacework that had graced the verandah, and a coronet on the roof, were long gone. The slate roof was now galvanised iron and the rooms were extremely dark and gloomy. Even for a Victorian home this gloom was depressing and unnecessary. The light globes we inherited were of such low wattage that for the first nights spent there in a rough camping-out sort of way, it was necessary to use a torch to read.

Still, as the agent had so rightly pointed out, it might be shabby and unloved, but all was not lost, it had not been destroyed. Just look at the cedar skirting boards and the one or two remaining ornamental ceilings. It was a renovator's delight.

So I proceeded to renovate, not once but twice, and it was during the second renovation that the new wing was built. Without being fanatically dictated to by 1881 detail, I tried to ensure that the new extension would be as sympathetic as possible to the original house. So room dimensions and joinery were duplicated, though the local Dungog cedar could no longer be used. Bricks were made of the same

size and colour as the originals, bay windows and chimneys faithfully
copied, and when the work was completed in 1994 the house had
been transformed into a truly gracious and comfortable home,
exceeding all my dreams. The most exciting part, to my mind, was the
addition of a walled area to become a garden, attached to the lower
west wall.

A view to the house from the Bright Border

The Garden

PHOTOGRAPHS of the house and its surrounds taken in 1989 show a Hills hoist, a brick and iron garage, scattered trees – mainly gums – and an old slab building at the back used for foaling. This home yard was fenced off with barbwire slung through timber posts, and the area beyond, to the creek, was divided into paddocks for cattle.

The garden was made up of mown grass, geraniums, a stunted frangipani (*Plumeria rubra* var. *acuminata*) near the verandah, and a passionfruit vine over the hen house. The best things were a mature silky oak near the kitchen, a gnarled camphor laurel full of wattlebirds and parrots, and a single bunya bunya, yesterday's landmark tree, planted near homesteads in the old days to help travellers find their way.

During the first renovation, in 1990, I had had a network of gravel paths laid at the back of the house. This was the most natural place to start as it faced north and was sheltered and sunny. The shaded front was too difficult for me to contemplate at that stage. I would work on it later.

These paths divided the back area into two large squares. The other important feature that we built here was a long pergola joining the house to a little guest building, known as The Cabins, fifty metres to the north.

It was Easter 1991 when I began to plant. I could not have articulated then, as I think I can now, what I was trying to do. I was simply doing what I had seen my mother do and her mother as well, using cuttings and seeds, jumbled together, filling every square inch.

ON NOT GROWING NATIVES

Hymenosporum flavum, the native frangipani, grows straight and tall to about fifteen metres, with dark glossy foliage and in spring the most sweetly scented cream-coloured frangipani-like flowers. They are not messy, and the perfume is out of this world. If only they could be brought to the attention of local councils, they would make excellent street trees. Two grow near the kitchen door and hold the distinction of being a rarity in this garden – Australian natives.

The lack of native plants had to be pointed out to me, for I certainly had no deliberate intent along these lines, and take little notice of plant origins, simply planting what I like.

Out on the farm and in the tree lanes I have planted thousands of eucalypts and wattles, and scores of melaleucas, hakeas, bottlebrushes and grevilleas, but it was not until it was remarked upon that I realised I had drawn a line around the garden, as if to say, 'Natives, advance no further.'

After thinking long and hard, I realised that within the garden I had planted many native plants, but they for one reason or another did not like living there; for the most part they had shrivelled up and died or become ugly and spindly. There was no conspiracy. Exceptions are the Gymea lilies at the front, a very pretty lillypilly, and a Geraldton wax whose soft pink flowers are exquisite in a bouquet. I confess to finding some wildflowers a bit garish and the foliage spiky and lacking softness. Kangaroo paw fits this category. That is a plant I have no desire to grow. Waratahs, flannel flowers and Christmas bells are of great sentimental attachment, but they would never grow here in this soil, and I have killed more Christmas bush than I care to think about.

At the risk of incurring the wrath of native-plant enthusiasts, all I can say is that with the exception of one splendid local Dungog garden, I find an overuse of native plants a bit dull and boring. They are not really suited to my mixed beds anyway, because of the soil conditions they prefer. As my preferences do not seem to upset the wildlife, I don't see why they should upset anyone else.

The Design

THE GARDEN evolved one bit at a time around the house, and as the house grew, so did the garden in its turn.

The Cottage Garden, with its intersecting paths, was the first and only area mapped out on paper. After this, each new garden came into being almost by accident.

The Big Vegetable Garden was created in the space that existed between The Cabins and the tennis court. I remember designing the beds using hoses laid out in various shapes on the ground. Most of the gardens after that were designed by the tomato-stake method, which involves simply getting a bundle of stakes, laying them on the ground to form patterns, and moving them about until it looks right. It was not until James came along that a tape measure and string line were used.

Some might think that making a garden this way, a bit at a time without an overall scheme in mind, is too risky, that mistakes will probably be made that will have to be redone, and the garden may very well end up a hotchpotch of unrelated elements. That is the risk. On the other hand, there are very good reasons why this garden would not exist at all if a grand scheme had had to be produced right at the start and why I strongly recommend doing things a bit at a time.

The most important reason is to do with husbands. If in the early days my husband, Rob, had caught a mere glimmer of what was going to eventuate, I think he might have tied me to a very large rock and flung me in the dam. Some things need to awaken slowly to the consciousness. I'm not saying I was devious, for I hardly knew what was happening myself, but as all gardeners know, if there are no fences, no boundaries, no limits, one just keeps on digging.

He used to say to me 'Don't make it so big you can't look after it', and I always thought I could. I didn't set out deliberately to create a rod for my own back, for I was strong and healthy and I loved outdoor work. I think it was the day the semi-trailer arrived full of agapanthus and murrayas (orange jessamine) that he started to get worried and we had our first big argument. He was rational but wrong and I was very emotional and right and we turned a very important corner. Beauty had won the day. It had seeped into his bones, and become important for its own sake.

There is also the expense of gardening to consider. A large design means a large expense, all at once. The garden would not exist if I had had to call in the professional landscapers. The cost, quite simply, would have been prohibitive.

So it was designed over a period of time, mainly of an evening by lots of wanderings about with glass of wine·in hand, contemplating the space, and then playing about with it until it felt right. The most important thing was not being afraid and remembering I had no-one to please but myself – and Rob.

THE COTTAGE GARDEN

This was the first garden made, and is still my favourite. It is the heart of the garden where I am most truly at home and happiest. It began under the camphor laurel and is much changed since the first modest plantings of diosma and petunias. The diosmas all died and petunias would now be out of place.

In the shady parts are dwarf arum lilies and clivias, plectranthus and violets. In the dappled shade are heliotropes, aquilegias and autumn crocus and in spring, white foxgloves and primulas, soft yellow pansies, white ranunculus and, around the stepping stones, sweet alyssum and dwarf nasturtiums.

The large sunny squares are filled with a mixed planting of shrubs, bulbs, perennials, annuals and some climbers. There is no particular colour scheme, but there might be leanings toward pink in one corner, or oranges and yellows in another.

Where paths intersect we have made graceful arches out of metal rods – rio, used more commonly for reinforcing concrete. Over these clamber a pink clematis and the roses 'Blackboy', 'Blossomtime' and 'Lamarque'.

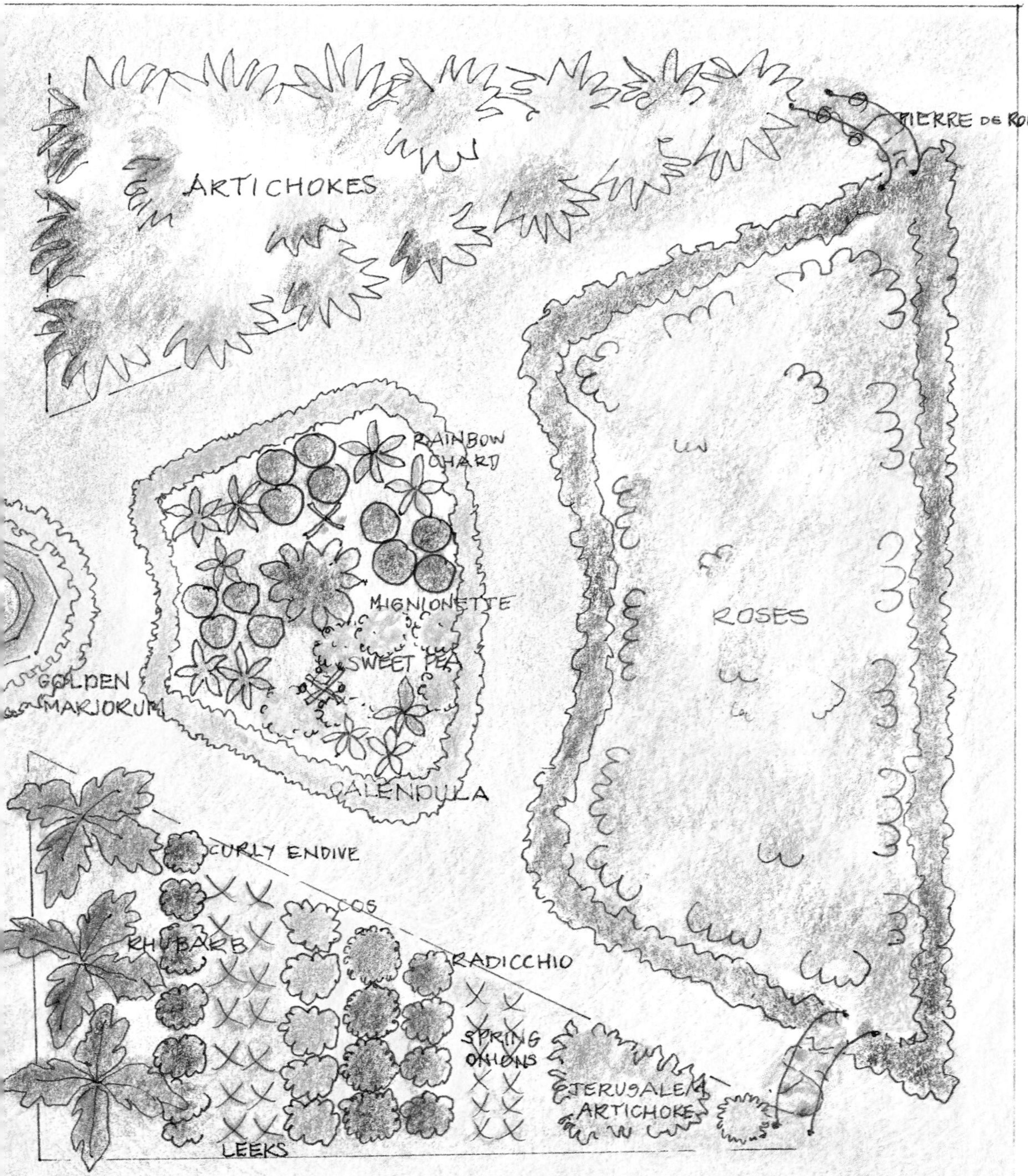

ARTICHOKES

PIERRE DE RONS

RAINBOW
CHARD

GOLDEN
MARJORUM

MIGNIONETTE

SWEET PEA

ROSES

CALENDULA

CURLY ENDIVE

COS

RHUBARB

RADICCHIO

SPRING
ONIONS

JERUSALEM
ARTICHOKE

LEEKS

GARDEN

THE HERB GARDEN

Rosemary, thyme, oregano, parsley – both flat and curly – chives, various mints, dill, basil and sage. These are the herbs I mostly cook with. I have become particularly fond of the spicy globe basil, which clumps up nicely into thick mounds and lasts for months on end, much longer than the larger-leafed variety. It is so easy to grow that I have started using it, as I do parsley and chives, to make borders. Borage, chamomile, horseradish and wild fennel are grown for their interesting leaves and flowers. I'm not inclined to monk-like activities such as making teas and medicinal concoctions and I wouldn't, even if there were more hours in the day. There are enough things to do.

That leaves the curry plant, which like all silvery things will die if it gets too wet. I never give up and replant it every year like an annual. The heavy lingering scent of curry in the air is too intriguing to forgo for a little difficulty.

Finally, there are the flowers: violas, nasturtiums and the whole lot hedged with autumn crocus.

THE BIG VEGETABLE GARDEN

This is glimpsed from the Cottage Garden, through the long wisteria walkway. At its centre is a raised pond filled with deep blue water iris and surrounded by a thick carpet of golden oregano. The beds are laid out to form a pattern, and grassed pathways all lead to this pond.

As there is very little topsoil above the heavy clay, the beds are raised about twenty centimetres and are in a constant state of being built up with compost and manure. At each end of the Big Vegetable Garden are two large rosebeds edged with catmint. In spring sweetpeas climb home-made bamboo teepees in-between cabbages and mixed salads. Calendulas alternate with marigolds to make floral borders around vegetables. Some purists may well shake their heads at this – and they do – but I would no more grow vegetables without companion flowers than I would only grow them in straight rows. I've never really understood why straight rows are essential to a vegetable planting, and enjoy tossing seeds about in drifts and circles – anything, just as long as it's not straight.

Crops are rotated, allowing used beds to rest for a while and rejuvenate with copious additions of blood and bone and poultry manure and anything else we can lay hands on. Carrots, snowpeas, peas, beans of all kinds, brussels sprouts, spinach, silverbeet, onions, leeks and shallots take turns according to the seasons. Globe artichokes are grown for the beauty of their leaves and flowers rather than the eating. My favourite rocket is always to be found. It is nice to

HERB GARDEN

let it flower and go to seed. The soft antique cream-coloured petals look marvellous against the leaves of giant mustard, and the seeds are easily harvested for another day's planting.

THE LITTLE VEGETABLE GARDEN

On the other side of the orchard, near the hens and pig, are the smaller beds for beetroot, tomatoes, eggplant, sweetcorn, capsicums, more peas and beans, celery and strawberries. Chokos and raspberries scramble up wire frames. Here we grow more flowers for cutting: sunflowers, which the cockatoos usually demolish, and gladiolus. I think this must be James's favourite spot, for he is often to be found here, and it's always as neat as a pin. He has created wonderful frames of bamboo and rio, and the vegetables, set out ornamentally and edged with borders of parsley and chives, are so pretty a picture that it's a pity to pull them out to eat.

THE WALLED GARDEN

This enclosed space, with its raised octagonal pond at the centre, has the feeling of a cloister. Apart from the twitterings of tiny birds in the mop-top robinias, all is quiet. The high brick walls lend an air of privacy to what is hidden away inside. It is a garden to come to for solitude. I often visit when I feel a little depressed or worried about something and just sit still for a while, in the hope of regaining serenity and a sense of balance.

Around the pond lies a small formal garden planted with the deep-blue bearded iris 'Venetian Waters' and surrounded by a neatly clipped English box border. A brick path divides these beds from the wider border where a more exuberant planting lies, of buddleias and salvias intermingled with canterbury bells, in season, foxgloves and cleome. Standard 'Iceberg' roses give form and 'The Fairy' rose underplanted with catmint at the edge, softness.

The colours are deliberately soft and harmonious, shades of blue, pink and white. The marble maidens come from an old church at Rye on England's south coast. Holding anchors, if somewhat damaged with the years, they tell of life once near the sea. An equally old bell house stands at the far wall and, behind it, the splendid pink climbing rose 'Mme Grégoire Staechelin'.

THE BRIGHT BORDER

These colourful beds lead to the Walled Garden, but up until two years ago they were not even dreamed of. That is, not until the dog yard was made. Time and again I have found that taking one step leads logically and almost inevitably to the next. I acquired the

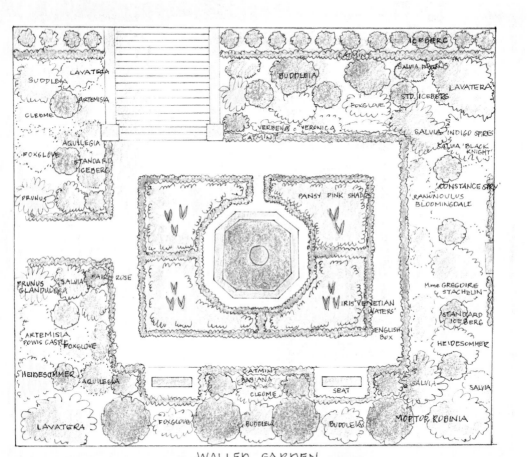

ICEBERG

LAVATERA
BUDDLEIA
ARTEMISIA
CLEOME
BUDDLEIA
SALVIA PATENS
STD. ICEBERG
LAVATERA
FOXGLOVE
AQUILEGIA
STANDARD ICEBERG
VERBENA VERONICA
CATMINT
SALVIA INDIGO SPIRES
SALVIA 'BLACK KNIGHT'
FOXGLOVE
PRUNUS

PANSY PINK SHADES
'CONSTANCE SPRY'
RANUNCULUS BLOOMINGDALE

PRUNUS GLANDULOSA
SALVIA FAIR ROSE
Mme GREGOIRE STAECHELIN
STANDARD ICEBERG
ARTEMISIA POWIS CASTLE
FOXGLOVE
IRIS 'VENETIAN WATERS'
ENGLISH BOX
HEIDESOMMER
HEIDESOMMER
AQUILEGIA

CATMINT
BABIANA
CLEOME
SEAT
SALVIA
SALVIA
LAVATERA
FOXGLOVE
BUDDLEIA
BUDDLEIAS
MOPTOP ROBINIA

WALLED GARDEN

puppies, the dog yard had to be built to restrain their wanderings, and there we were, with a perfect edge along which to make another garden bed!

What I wanted to do here was to make a garden of intense colour, bright yellows and oranges, hectic purples and reds. There were two reasons. It would contrast with what lay beyond in the soft calm of the Walled Garden and, perhaps most importantly, I knew my husband would like it. I have many theories about men. One is that most of them like custard; another, that they like bright colours, particularly when it comes to flowers. So many women plant pastels and have a thing about white gardens. All the men I know find this very boring so I decided to make this new garden a place that they would love.

It is a garden one comes upon suddenly. You round a bend, and there it is – all dazzling and luminous and fun. Poppies of every kind dominate the spring planting, with strawflowers, old-fashioned snapdragons, penstemons, poached-egg plant, green Irish bells, delphiniums, bidens, bright yellow pansies, and red and orange ranunculus. As summer approaches these give way to zinnias, geums, cosmos, and dwarf lemon sunflowers. Clumps of yellow Dutch iris, dwarf orange cannas and deep blue and purple salvias give height and form all year round.

THE FRONT GARDEN

The Front Garden faces south and is dark and cold for much of the year. Here are massed agapanthus of blue and white, clivia, arum lilies, acanthus, hostas, helleborus and plectranthus, with lamiums along edges and under trees. To the west, where there is increased light, the plantings change to heliotropes, hydrangeas, astilbe, daisies, comfrey, bog sage, the 'Green Ice' rose and Californian poppies, including a purple one.

In the centre of the drive is a teardrop-shaped garden full of yellow. Yellow lantanas, both upright and prostrate, and tagetes, which I like, but no one else does because it can cause rash at pruning time. There is a clump of tall yellow cannas at the centre and Gymea lilies here and there.

Here at the front the colours are predominantly blue, yellow and orange with a touch of white. Pink would look out of place against the orange bricks, while these sunny colours help dispel the gloom.

THE YELLOW ROSE GARDEN

The other important garden is the Yellow Rose Garden. Anxiety almost saw me carried off when this was made. It looked terrible – the concrete footing, the circle of poisoned grass. I was asked if it was a landing pad for helicopters, or aliens. The brick wall looked so big and ugly that I wanted it torn down immediately. This was a time to sit in the walled garden and think calming thoughts.

Now that it is filled with mature healthy roses, catmint and dwarf nasturtiums at the edge, a Japanese box hedge all around and a beautiful, soft yellow-tinted urn at the centre, I feel much better. It is a perfect focal point at the end of the Long Walk – an avenue of liquidambars, sapiums and jacarandas in the front park. At the other end is another fine urn decorated with mermaids.

The Yellow Rose Garden was almost the death of me. Alongside the drive, it is the first thing you see as you approach the house. Now I can't imagine how we did without it.

THE ROSE GARDEN

The Rose Garden came into being not so much from an abiding love of roses, but a need for order and symmetry and something different after the hectic profusion of the Cottage Garden beds. These two gardens sit side by side, separated by a double hedge of murraya and plumbago and accessed by a hoopway smothered in the small white single thornless 'Rose of Japan'.

The four, large, square beds were laid out with intersecting grass walkways – using the tomato-stake method – dug and mulched and finally contemplated. What would I plant? Definitely not more cottage plants – that would not be logical, for a garden needs points of contrast, not just more of the same. Our success with roses up roadways, along fences, in the Big Vegetable Garden and other areas encouraged me to keep going.

So these first four beds were filled, for the first time according to a colour scheme – white, pink, yellow and apricot, and red. Later four pergolas were added for 'Albertine' and 'New Dawn' to scramble over, and three more beds, this time, mixed colours. Most recently extra rose tunnels have been added and planted with 'Mme Alfred Carrière'. At either end of these tunnels sit wire seats, so secluded that the occupant, sitting ever so still, will experience at close quarters the comings and goings of blue wrens as they hop in and out of neighbouring hedges. This is where I sometimes hide from the world with only the dogs able to find me.

Of particular note in the apricot bed, 'Leander' is vigorous, sending out arching sprays of massed perfumed flowers. I love the strangely green-tinged yellow rose 'Lanvin' and, of the pink ones, 'Belle Story', 'Mary Rose', 'Gertrude Jekyll' and 'Pretty Jessica'. They are all beautiful.

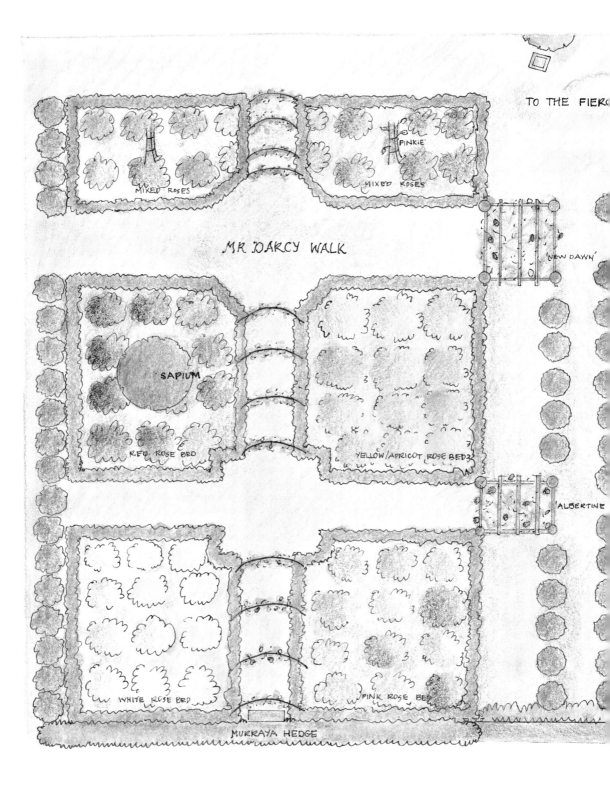

TO THE FIEL

MIXED ROSES

'PINKIE'

MIXED ROSES

'NEW DAWN'

MR DARCY WALK

SAPIUM

RED ROSE BED

YELLOW/APRICOT ROSE BEDS

'ALBERTINE'

WHITE ROSE BED

PINK ROSE BED

MURRAYA HEDGE

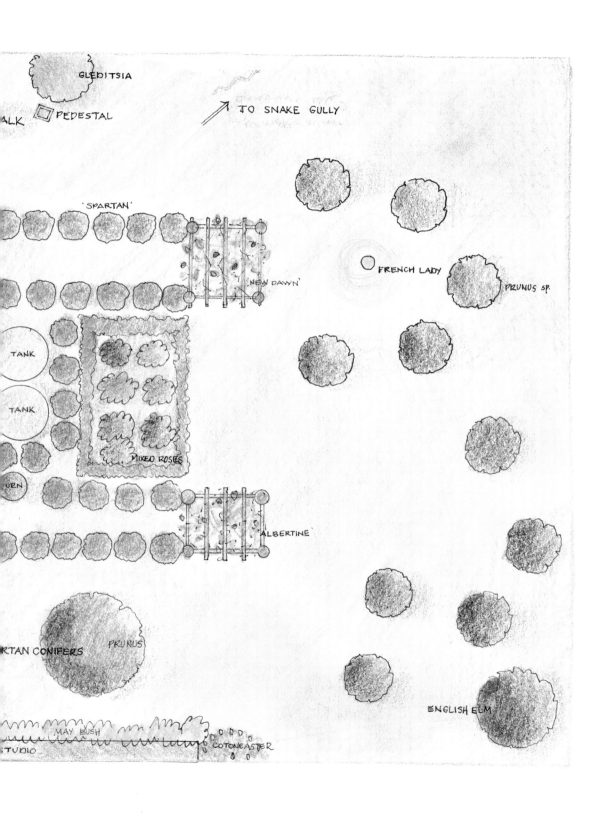

SNAKE GULLY AND THE FIERCE WALK

I first walked in Snake Gully when it was knee-high in paspalum grass and separated from the house yard by a barbwire fence. It seemed a very long way away, everything wild and overgrown, nothing more than a cow paddock running along the creek. I never dreamed in those days that it would be part of a garden. Here I encountered the first of many snakes shocked out of their peaceful existence by all my comings and goings.

The summer house came from my old home in Sydney. We pulled it to pieces and reconstructed it beside the creek, dug garden beds around it, including several more for roses, and planted poplars, jacarandas and a wonderful Powton tree nearby. Later came the steps where griffins stand guard, and the rest of the Fierce Walk leading back, past the headless monk and other frights, to the formal, civilised safety of the Rose Garden.

Despite the fierce creatures that line the way, snakes and other intimations of danger, Snake Gully has an atmosphere of complete repose, always cool and green, the air filled with gentle whisperings from the creek. It is another place to sit and observe nature, particularly water dragons, rabbits on the far bank, and coots and ducks splashing about among the reeds. It is a pity the platypus has not been sighted for four years.

Facing page: Looking towards the Vegetable Garden from the Cottage Garden

The Design

garden

A Year at Torryburn:

notes and food

January

Listless, languid, lazy, lolling about reading books given for Christmas. I'm ignoring the garden temporarily.

So entangled in a neighbouring buddleia that I almost missed seeing it, the snail creeper is curiously intricate and full of heady perfume like honey. The ants like it too, swarming about deep inside the flowers.

Tall zinnias, with their luminous paintbox colours, make the Bright Border bright all over again. Then there is lythrum (loosestrife) flowering virtually all summer, tough and pretty with its fluffy lilac–pink flowers.

I'm collecting hollyhock seeds, snipping off stems and laying them on sheets of newspaper on the dining-room table. One is my mother's single pink, which is especially important to save – a part of her to plant each year.

These months of summer we lay under a blanket of heat. We – me and the plants – concentrate on surviving. With late summer rains and near tropical humidity the grass grows before our eyes. You can smell it. The days are consumed with mowing and the air is so filled with the din of cicadas that we have to shout at each other to be heard.

Today eleven palm trees – six Canary Island and five cabbage palms – arrived on the back of an enormous truck. An excavator dug holes, a tractor carried soil, two men wielded spades and, as if that wasn't enough, a backhoe scooped out trenches ready for the arrival of two cement trucks to pour footings for three new gardens.

I ran about with a camera, iced cordial and sandwiches, feeling as a film director must in the middle of an epic movie, waving arms – and legs – and spurring others along. This sort of gardening is fun, as fully grown trees move through the air on slings with all the action and drama, suspense and timing of a military operation.

My sister now has faith that we have not lost the ability to build pyramids. Never has there been so much machinery and so much happening here on one day and, as if to cheer us, cool misty rain fell on the new trees overnight.

THE SNAKE

One of the realities of living in the Australian countryside is living with snakes – most of them extremely venomous. This doesn't worry me in the slightest, for they are much more vulnerable than I am. Indeed, I feel sorry for them and the horror with which most people regard them. Like most wild animals they are timid and keep to themselves; only occasionally stumbling upon one another, as we must in a garden as wild as this and bounded by a creek.

It was late in the month and James was working in one of the thickly planted cottage beds, intent on re-staking a top-heavy weeping 'Dorothy Perkins'. Standing knee-deep in nasturtiums and salvias and avoiding the tangle of thorn-laden stems, he manhandled the rose into some sort of order and stepped back to have a better look.

Following him out of the undergrowth, hard upon his thickly booted heels, came a very large brown snake which, when it realised that the other moving object was a gardener, quickly disappeared, this time into the safe haven of the periwinkle under the grapefruit tree.

The next day, periwinkle gave way beneath our mattocks and we stamped about noisily hoping to frighten whatever lay thereabouts back down to the creek. Of course there was nothing.

The brown snake had shown itself before this – a shed skin near the laundry, an encounter while sipping tea on the verandah step and him – or is it her? – just behind me all coiled up and well camouflaged: brown snake on brown boards beside the brown doormat. We stumbled upon each other the following summer near the rhubarb.

One sweltering day a few weeks after our attack on the periwinkle, I arrived as usual with cat, dogs, Esky, boxes of groceries. Everything still and sultry – perfect snake weather, so I thought, shepherding the dogs through the house and letting them into the restricted safety of the dog yard, to run around while I unpacked. This yard stops them running through wilder parts of the garden and down to the creek, which is far too dangerous at this time of year.

Excited barking brought me back to the door where I could see the silly pair standing over a snake, disturbed, it seemed, from a leisurely siesta on the lawn. I could see neither its head nor the end of its tail, only the windings of its long thick body across the grass. I knew that if I rushed out of that door with the snake between me and the dogs they would attack it instinctively, so back I ran, through the house and right around the garden to the other side of the yard, calling them in the opposite direction, absolutely amazed when they obeyed me. Then I grabbed a spade and went in search, all trembling. This was a gesture of defiance more than any real threat, either to me or the snake. I'm sure it headed for the hills the minute it was so rudely awoken.

It might seem strange, but for all my heart flutterings and anxious moments, I'm not sorry that things are the way they are. I'm certain we will stumble across one another again one day, always unexpectedly. Paradise has its serpent. This one has attained mythical proportions. As each spring approaches I anticipate the first sighting, not of buds or swallows, but snakes, and I know my silent, bright-eyed friend will not be far away.

ROSES

I never knew what it was to grow roses until I came to Torryburn. Apart from the 'Cécile Brunner' which, in partnership with asparagus fern, was an important component of posy making, they form no part of my childhood garden memories. Rose growing was a mystery, with a distinct aura of difficulty. What I have discovered is how forgiving and tough a plant a rose can be, even in the hands of a rank amateur. Once started, it is impossible not to be hooked. Now I have planted at least a thousand.

I love to pile them into vases, all mixed up, colours and varieties, just as they grow in the garden, 'Jane Austen', 'Mary Rose' and 'Leander' right alongside 'Peace', 'Double Delight' and 'First Prize'.

My favourite shades would have to be the pale pinks and apricots, but others – like Rob – prefer red, and I have to agree that 'Mr Lincoln' is the king when it comes to perfume. I have found blue roses to be impossible and gave up after numerous attempts, watching 'Blue Moon' sicken and die long ago. On the other hand, the purple and deep violet shades prosper.

Perhaps because we enjoy a fairly dry heat in summer, lots of open sunshine well away from large shady trees, and because the plantings in and around the roses are so diverse, we have few of the usual problems with aphids and black spot. Still, we spray the roses with white oil to prevent thrip and recently when red spider mites began to infest the beds in Snake Gully, we bought predatory mites to control the problem in a natural way. The mites arrived by post in a jar full of leaves, and we simply scattered them about under the worst-affected bushes. The soil is fed from time to time with sulphate of potash, and the usual mixture used throughout the garden that I call the pudding mix – blood and bone, pelleted chicken manure, fresh horse and cow manure and mushroom compost. Lucerne hay is scattered about on top as mulch.

If I could only have one rose in my garden I think it would be 'Charles Austin' for its interesting form from bud to full-blown flower, the softest apricot-tinged buds opening to a lighter pink, and its full fruity fragrance. Also I find that like many of the old-fashioned English roses of David Austin, it is tough and easy to grow here in the Hunter.

Along with the bearded iris, and sweet old-fashioned violets, roses are my great love. It will soon be that time of year when the rose catalogues appear and it will be time to select some new ones and worry later about where they will be planted.

Summer pasta

Nothing equals the taste of freshly rolled and cooked pasta. Summer holidays bring family visitors to stay and one day I entertained them, children and all, with pasta-making lessons.

Basic Pasta

Enough for 4 people as a small course or as a side accompaniment to a main dish. I use a small Imperial noodle-making machine to roll out the dough and cut the pasta and find it makes the work very easy indeed. Of course, you can do it by hand.

210 g (7½ oz) plain flour
2 eggs
¼ teaspoon salt

BY MACHINE
Sift the flour and salt into a food processor. Break in the eggs and combine with an on/off motion until the mixture resembles breadcrumbs. Tip the mixture out onto the workbench and knead for several minutes until the dough feels smooth and pliable.

BY HAND
Sift the flour and salt in a heap onto the workbench. Make a well in the centre and break the eggs in. Mix the eggs, bit by bit, into the flour until everything is well combined, then knead.

▶ Cut the dough into two pieces, and working each separately, commence at the widest margin and knead the dough through the pasta machine 2 or 3 times. Gradually adjust and narrow the rolling margin, and when the pasta has been rolled to the finest point, cut the sheets in half. This makes the handling a lot easier. Now pass the sheets through the cutting section, and spread the noodles out on a tray or hang on wire coathangers until needed. It may be necessary to loosen them a little with your hands lightly dusted with flour.
▶ Cook in boiling salted water until done. This will take only a couple of minutes. Drain and serve immediately with sauce or topping of choice.

▶ Prepare pasta dough as on page 31. Slice the ball in half and work with only half at a time. Roll out the dough into a long rectangular strip, as thinly as possible. Cut the strip in half. Lay one strip on a lightly floured workbench and dot with heaped teaspoonfuls of the filling (see pages 33–34) at equal distances. I usually make two ravioli at a time by placing double rows of mixture close together, side by side. Flatten the mixture with the back of a spoon and place the other half strip of pasta over the top. Press down well and cut out squares around each mound of filling, using a crinkly pie cutter. Repeat the procedure with the remaining piece of dough. Place the finished ravioli on a lightly floured tray, to prevent sticking until you are ready to cook them. Alternatively they can be placed on sheets of foil and put into the freezer.

▶ Cook by boiling in copious amounts of boiling salted water for 10 minutes. Drain well.

Pumpkin Ravioli with Parmesan, Butter and Sage

1 quantity ravioli dough (page 31)
6 tablespoons melted butter
handful sage leaves, finely sliced

FILLING
2 cups (18 fl oz) cooked, well-drained pumpkin (requires approximately
    800 g/1¾ lb raw, peeled pumpkin)
knob of butter
black pepper and salt

▶ Mash hot pumpkin with butter and add salt and freshly ground
black pepper. Prepare the ravioli (as previous recipe). Cook by boiling
in copious amounts of salted water for 10 minutes, or until tender. As
the ravioli are delicate, what I do is to bring the water to the boil, put
in the ravioli and reduce the heat to more of a simmer, so that they
are not violently tossed about during the cooking. During a too-
vigorous boil, they are likely to split open and lose their filling.
Drain well.

▶ To serve, melt enough butter for the number of serves cooked and
add a handful of finely sliced sage to the pan. When butter is sizzling,
and just before the point of burning, pour over the ravioli. Sprinkle
with freshly grated parmesan.

January

Goat's Cheese Ravioli with Tomato Cream

1 quantity ravioli dough (see recipe page 32)

FILLING
450 g (1 lb) goat's cheese
little cream
handful finely sliced chives

TOMATO CREAM
1 litre (1¾ pints) fresh tomato purée, sieved to remove seeds
salt and black pepper
½ cup (4 tablespoons) finely sliced basil leaves
250 ml (9 fl oz) cream

▶ Make filling: mash goat's cheese with cream until soft, then add chives. Make ravioli with the filling.

▶ For the tomato cream, reduce the purée until thick. Season with salt and black pepper to taste. Add basil. Finish with cream and reduce further to sauce consistency.

▶ The ravioli can be cooked and placed in a lightly buttered casserole dish, the sauce spooned over, and set aside until ready to serve by reheating in an oven until bubbling.

Frittata of Sweet Red Peppers, Herbs and Goat's Cheese

2 large potatoes, peeled, washed and grated
2 tablespoons extra-virgin olive oil
black pepper and salt
100 g (3½ oz) goat's cheese
1 red capsicum
125 ml (5 fl oz) honey
½ cup (4 tablespoons) mixed fresh herbs, chopped (I use basil, parsley
   and chives)
3 eggs
water

▶ Heat oil in a 20 cm (8 in) frying pan. Press the potato in. Cook until it is all stuck together and nice and brown underneath. Turn over to cook the potato thoroughly. Turn back over again. Grind pepper and salt all over.

▶ Prepare red capsicum: blister over flame, peel and chop, then cook further in honey until soft.

▶ Scatter the capsicum and knobs of goat's cheese all over the potato, then the herbs. Beat the eggs with a little water and pour over. Cook until everything is pretty well set, then turn over to cook the top side a little more, just for a minute. (I hold a plate over the top of the frittata as I do the turning as everything is a bit too soft to trust to a spatula.)

▶ Serve potato-side up, and eat at once with a green salad.

Green Salad

▶ Put together a nice selection of fresh salad leaves, well washed and drained. In the garden we grow cos lettuce, radicchio, oakleaf lettuce, curly endive, English spinach and rocket. There is always rocket, baby seedlings coming up as older plants come into flower all year round. I like its mild nutty flavour combined with toasted pine nuts and the following Mustard Dressing.

Mustard Dressing

▶ Fill a screw-top glass jar about two-thirds full with extra-virgin olive oil. Top up the best part of what remains with balsamic vinegar. Add 2 teaspoonfuls sugar, 2 good tablespoons Dijon mustard, black pepper and salt to taste, and give a good shake. Taste and adjust the ingredients to suit.

Chilled Orange and Ginger Salad

Serves 4

4 nice oranges
2 tablespoons ginger in syrup, chopped finely
some finely shredded mint leaves

▶ Mix everything together and chill. Serve with cream.

February

THANK goodness it is overcast and cool. We have been cutting back the cottage beds. In late summer it is hard not to become impatient at the overgrown and straggly gardens. Where only a few months ago I longed for the garden to swell up to full blousiness, now I itch to trim and tidy. Somewhere in between lies the perfect balance between order and chaos.

The English lavender in the walled garden has been particularly beautiful. We have cut it all and made large bunches to hang upside-down along wires in the garage. Thousands of flowers drop everywhere. A most fragrant day's work.

A lot of my energy is sapped by worrying about farm staff and interviewing candidates for the Stud Master position which has once more fallen vacant. How I long for stability. The garden crew seem happy and are wonderful. James, whom I rely on to do all the really hard work, combines gardening with almost anything else – changing light globes, building garden sheds. He is a carpenter who now prefers to work with plants, in his own quietly organised way. What I need is someone like James to look after the horses.

The most exciting step forward has been creating the Wisteria Garden in the space between the house and the pool. This part of the garden has changed very little since the day we first came, a grassed area dotted with shrubs and trees. What troubled me most was the slope, for the garden I pictured in my mind's eye needed to be perfectly flat.

Out came the pegs and string lines to determine exactly what we were dealing with, and a lot of walking up and down trying to imagine how it might look. In the end I nervously decided on creating a low, brick, retaining wall with steps. This would lead up to a rectangle of perfectly flat turf, edged with what I hoped one day would be spectacular: wisteria trees to be seen from the kitchen window and delight all those employed in washing up. I wanted to be able to walk freely between each tree, so instead of a trellis framework we set about making individual poles of waterpipe with a cross of thinner pipe at the top to act as a support. Now that it is made, the overall effect is one of a futuristic power station, decidedly ugly and making me more nervous than ever. Everyone tells me to stop worrying.

The mail-order wisteria arrived and are damaged and disappointing. I do not have the strength to complain, but make a note to myself to buy elsewhere in future. I am beginning to lose my nerve and I wonder if it's because I am trying too hard, worried about what other people will think.

Autumn is in the air. Sometimes when I know it's morning and the garden is out there, I put on dressing gown and slippers and do a little digging before breakfast.

Cool mornings, swarms of swallows on the dam, masses of simple white flowers with yellow centres bursting open – autumn crocus. Some people mistake the clumps of crocus for chives and bring me handfuls to cook with. They make pretty borders around cottage and herb beds, down roadways, under roses, happy to be in full sun or shade, and thicken into dividable clumps very quickly. At the end of summer, just when you thought everything was tired and over, there it is.

GENEVIEVE THE PIG

Genevieve arrived in the back of a station wagon one February day three years ago. She was a very cute young pig, very pink, with a rubbery sort of nose like a trumpet. Her ears had notches clipped out of them, she was without a tail, and her little legs were misshapen and wobbly to walk on.

The people who had reared her from a tiny piglet were really sad at the thought of their imminent parting. She had grown up in their

home, and they would sorely miss watching her have fun skating up and down the polished boards in their hallway. But she was growing fast and a fully grown pig would have trouble fitting into suburban life. So she had come to live here on the farm. As a parting gift they had brought a box of bananas, a box of grapes, a nice stainless steel dinner bowl, a doona for her to sleep on, a pillow for extra comfort, and a towel for washing her face.

After I had been given many instructions, there was a tearful farewell, and Genevieve settled into her new home beside the hen house overlooking the creek. It was simply not possible to keep her looking as spruced as the day she arrived. The doona was soon shredded and dragged about in muddy strips, and the face washing was given up after the first couple of days. We tried getting her in a head lock, but quickly learned after some undignified struggles where the words 'pigroot' and 'pigheaded' come from.

Genevieve was one of five piglets taken by animal liberation supporters from a large piggery. Three were dead and two gravely ill. One of those was soon to die at a veterinary hospital, but the remaining one, Genevieve, her legs twisted from arthritis, survived. Since then, the ongoing actions of those caring people have resulted in new laws being introduced outlawing the use of iron collars on breeding sows.

Genevieve is now a large sow herself, though she will never have piglets. She is a gentle character, alert and sensitive. She recognises people, and spins about all grunts and flapping ears when she sees me coming with leftovers. She particularly likes apples, bananas, sticky date pudding, pasta and sponge cake. There is nothing quite to equal the sight of a pig eating a tub of ice cream, all froths and smiles.

Some may wonder what her life means now, living alone, this somewhat artificial existence, well past her intended live-by date, with only hens and birds and the occasional visitor, and the days and seasons passing by. One may very well wonder at the meaning of existence at all.

For me, Genevieve has become a symbol of some kind, of nature, of beasts, of part of ourselves. She certainly makes an impact on people when they meet her for the first time. They feel better for having patted her tough bristly head, for having put a bunch of grapes into her mouth and watched her slurp, for hosing her down so that she can make a mud pack from which she will emerge even pinker than ever.

Genevieve is a star, and she helps to heal the part of us that is sorry for helping to create the hell from which she came.

THE DISAPPEARING LEG OF LAMB

Life is difficult at times and nowhere more so than on a farm. One day I arrived, exhausted as usual, ready to settle down with a nice cup of tea and relax. The only problem was there was no water. The water comes from a tank and is brought to the house by means of an electric pump; the safety switch we had installed in the fuse box had tripped out, so with no electricity there was no water, and with no water, no tea.

What had caused the fuse to blow? Mice had chewed through the dishwasher cord. Now a terrible smell emanated from the refrigerator and freezer. Rotten meat. Luckily I had brought with me a leg of lamb. As it was frozen I left it on the sink to defrost, then went to lie down for a while to recover.

Dozing off, I awoke to a loud thud, blamed a thoughtless husband, drifted some more, then ran to the kitchen. Tiny muddy footprints dotted the sink and the lamb was gone. Not being one to give up easily I rallied help, a reluctant husband, found him a torch, and cheered him on, under the house in search of our dinner and the giant feral cat that lived there. Not without protest, on hands and knees he picked his way into the pitch-black labyrinth of brick footings festooned with dusty webs, home to rats, rabbits and snakes.

Half an hour passed, then another, and after many cryings out on my part, and no replies on his. I feared the worst and ran for help. I could see the headlines – man in pursuit of leg of lamb killed by cat.

Help arrived post haste in the form of a stable hand grinning from ear to ear. Nothing makes farm life more entertaining than our arrival and the incredible events that then take place. There was no lamb for dinner that night. Rob eventually emerged, pale with dust and cobwebs.

A couple of weeks later the giant cat was shot as it was seen dragging another pet cat by the scruff of its neck down a lane. And finally, weeks later, the bone from the leg of lamb was turned up by the plumber.

Leg of Lamb with Garlic, Rosemary and Polenta

Serves 6

1 x 2.5 kg (5 lb) leg of lamb
3 sprigs rosemary
2 cloves garlic, split lengthwise
drizzle of olive oil
small square aluminium foil
1 cup (9 fl oz) red wine
2 cups (18 fl oz) reduced veal stock (it's simplest to buy ready made, but I've
　 given a recipe on page 44)

▶ Preheat oven to 200°C (400°F). Put leg in roasting pan. Spike four holes into top side with knife point and insert garlic. Place 2 sprigs of rosemary on top, drizzle oil over, cover with foil, and roast for 2 hours. Take foil off after 1 hour.
▶ Leg should be pink in centre and juicy when done. Pour fat from pan and soak up extra grease with tissues.
▶ Return pan to hot plate, add chopped rosemary from the remaining sprig. Pour in the wine and boil rapidly until almost gone.
▶ Add veal stock, boil again until slightly thick. Pour into gravy boat.

Polenta

2½ cups (1 pint) water
½ teaspoon salt
125 g (4 oz) polenta
1 egg, beaten
180 g (6 oz) grated parmesan cheese

▶ Bring water and salt to the boil. Add the polenta and stir continuously until a soft porridge. Stir in the egg and 120 g (4 oz) cheese off the heat. Transfer mixture to oven dish and cover with remaining cheese. Bake at 200°C (400°F) until golden brown – approximately half an hour.
▶ Serve lamb and polenta with green beans and homemade gravy.

Poached Peaches with Strawberry and Honey Ice Cream (see recipe page 48)

February

Basic Veal Stock

5 kg (10 lb) sawn veal shanks (nice meaty pieces)
2–3 pig's trotters
3 leeks, white part only
3 large onions
3 large carrots
3 sticks celery
1 small bunch parsley
some fresh thyme sprigs
a bay leaf
1 ripe tomato
mushroom trimmings
1 teaspoon black peppercorns

▶ Wash the leeks, onions, carrots and celery and then chop into rough pieces. Make a bed of these in the bottom of a large baking pan. Spread the pieces of meat over the top and roast in a moderate oven (170–180°C, 325–350°F) until all is well browned but not black.

▶ Tip everything into a large stock pot. The bones and the vegetables, well packed, should fill it to about two-thirds. Deglaze the roasting pan very well with water, making sure you scrape up all the stuck-on bits, and add all the residual brown juices to the pot. (You can also use a little red or white wine to do this.) The deglazed juices help enormously to give the stock its lovely rich colour. Add the herbs, bits of mushroom, tomato and peppercorns and cover with lots of cold water. Bring to the boil, then adjust to a gentle simmer for about 8 hours (or overnight). From time to time skim the surface.

▶ Now strain the liquid through a sieve into another pot. Let it rest for a while, then ladle away any fat that settles on top. Boil rapidly to reduce by about half. Cool, then refrigerate. Any remaining fat will rise to the surface and solidify, making its removal very easy. You will now have a rich brown liquid ready for sauce making. This can be frozen until needed.

```
┌─────────────────────────────────────────────────┐
│                                                   │
│         A SUMMER DINNER FOR FOUR                   │
│                                                   │
│           CHILLED GREEN SOUP                       │
│                 DAMPER                             │
│                    •                              │
│           CHICKEN WITH BEANS                       │
│         ZESTY MASHED POTATOES                      │
│                    •                              │
│     POACHED PEACHES WITH STRAWBERRIES             │
│           AND HONEY ICE CREAM                      │
│                                                   │
└─────────────────────────────────────────────────┘
```

Chilled Green Soup

1 Spanish onion
2 large green capsicums
2 large Lebanese cucumbers
1 medium bunch coriander
3 ripe avocados
1 lemon
black pepper and salt
chopped chives, for garnish

▶ Put the onion, capsicums and cucumbers through a juicer. Transfer the juice to a blender and add coriander and 1 cup of water, then blend in avocados to thicken and then the lemon juice, pepper and salt to taste. More water can be added to adjust the consistency.
▶ Serve topped with greshly chopped chives.

300 g (11 oz) self-raising flour
½ teaspoon baking powder
pinch of salt
25 g (scant 1 oz) butter
2 tablespoons boiling water
200 ml (7 fl oz) milk

▶ Preheat oven to very hot, 240°C (470°F). Sift the flour, baking powder and salt into a bowl. Melt the butter in the boiling water, add to the milk, then mix with the dry ingredients to form a soft dough. Pat the dough into a round flat loaf about 20 cm (8 in) across. Bake for 15 minutes, then reduce the temperature to 200°C (400°F) for a further 5 minutes.

Chicken with Beans

2 small chickens
flour
black pepper and salt
extra-virgin olive oil for frying
4 rashers bacon, fat and rind removed, and chopped into dice
1 onion, peeled and chopped
1 clove garlic, minced
500 g (1 lb) assorted mushrooms
dry white wine
2 x 425 g (15 oz) cans diced tomatoes
2 sticks celery, sliced
300 g (11 oz) dried beans (e.g. kidney beans) soaked overnight, then simmered
    until tender
1 chopped tablespoon fresh rosemary
chopped parsley

► Section the chicken into joints. Dredge the pieces in flour, season with salt and pepper and fry in oil until golden. Put to one side.
► In a flameproof casserole fry the bacon pieces, onion and garlic together until done. Add the mushrooms and cook through.
► Add the wine and bring to the boil for a few minutes. Put in the tomatoes, celery, beans, rosemary and chicken pieces and simmer until the chicken is tender and the sauce is thickened. Serve topped with freshly chopped parsley.

This is a good dish to make the day before and reheat when needed.

Zesty Mashed Potatoes

► Make mashed potatoes as usual using butter, milk, cream, salt and black pepper to taste, and add some finely chopped parsley, 1 clove minced garlic and some lemon zest.

Poached Peaches with Strawberries and Honey Ice Cream

4 peaches (1 per person)
225 g (8 oz) sugar
water
2 punnets (500 g/1 lb) strawberries
extra 120 g (4 oz) sugar

ICE CREAM
4 egg yolks
3 tablespoons honey
375 ml (13 fl oz) cream

▶ To make ice cream, whisk the egg yolks and honey together until thick and creamy. Scald the cream and pour slowly onto the yolk mixture. Put everything back into the saucepan and cook gently, stirring all the while, until the mixture thickens. Cool and churn.

▶ Put the peaches into a large pan, cover with water, add the 225 g (8 oz) sugar, and bring to the boil. Simmer gently, until tender enough for the point of a sharp knife to pierce through to the stone easily. When done, hold under cold water to peel off the skins. Place in a bowl with some of the cooking syrup, to serve.

▶ Hull, then slice the strawberries into a bowl. Stir the extra sugar through and leave to stand at room temperature for a couple of hours (or until the juices begin to run).

March

WINDFLOWERS and sedums. This is an odd time of year and it is easy to forget what will happen next. The sedums cluster in a damp sunny corner of the cottage beds. They are succulents, which for much of the year appear as insignificant rosettes on top of the soil, until the end of summer when they shoot out their colourful flowers. Windflowers, which look half dead most of the time, suddenly appear in full health and bud, and I always wonder why I didn't plant more. There is brilliant purple with Tibouchina, and under the camphor laurel Plectranthus sends up delicate white spires. Autumn has its flowers, but they are not the ones we easily remember.

Under the camphor laurel there had always existed a pocket handkerchief of lawn. As shrubs grew and brought more shade, it became increasingly bare and alternatives to grass, like native violets, could not survive the constant stream of tramping feet. Now we are digging it all up with the idea of making a hard pebble surface with some sort of a pattern. A nice place to put a shady seat.

The morning to complete the job is now upon me: a circle of cement has been laid in preparation and I still haven't worked out a pattern. James has covered the circle with a cement glue, then spread more wet cement on top, all smooth and ready for me to start sticking in pebbles. These I bought in bags already sorted into their various colours: white, red and a deep blue–grey. Ingenious as always, James hammered a nail through the end of a piece of timber and, using this as a compass, drew a series of concentric circles intersected by lines as the basis for the design. I completed the design freehand, using a stick to draw curves and flowers. Balancing a plank across piled bricks at each end, in order to raise it off the ground, we are able to crawl on hands and knees out and over the wet cement and begin pressing in the stones.

What a job! It took three of us all day, and with caked-dry hands from handling the wet cement, aching knees and back and tired muscles, I began to wonder who dreamed up this idea. That is, until the next day, when the whole thing was hosed down, and we all looked very pleased with ourselves. 'We could say it is an archaeological relic we've just dug up.' Some of the stones that were not stuck in very well washed away, giving it an instant antique look, but the overall effect was there. Hardly a mosaic from the Alhambra, but good enough to keep us smiling.

This is a month of preparation. All the old tomato vines are pulled out and two cups of sugar per square metre spread around suspect areas to get rid of nematodes. Seed beds are prepared, manured and raked, eighty kilos of blood and bone put around the garden, and indoors, to get away from the smell, I am poring over nursery catalogues and writing out orders for bulbs, roses and perennials. I am also planning which annuals we will plant for spring and making lists. My mother used to say that I was born making a list – so I must be happy.

Autumn is the best time of year. Chill mornings, dew on the grass, and mist rising from the hollows. The light is softer, the mornings fresher, the sun mellower, the breezes gentler. It is a time when energy surges back into my being and I become hopeful all over again.

PLANTING TREES

Because the soil at Torryburn is so deficient – very thin topsoil on top of heavy clay – we grow new small trees on mounds of soil to get their roots off to a good start. Digging a hole meant that we were planting in what was virtually a clay pit and I have lost enough trees this way to inspire new ways of doing things and so far, the mound idea is proving to be the most successful.

The mound is mulched with stable straw and the roots watered in well with a liquid fertiliser. Wood chip was once used for mulch, but after a time we found that it set hard like concrete, preventing moisture from getting through at all. I also believe it leaches nutrients from the soil. Roundup is sprayed around the base of the mound to keep the grass at bay, and chicken-wire guards placed around the base of the tree to help protect against rabbits. Now all that is needed is a kookaburra to peck the tree in two or a large hare to stand on its hind

legs and nibble off the top. Tree planting is fraught with difficulty and a percentage of them can be guaranteed not to survive. I often wonder if the people who are so intent on cutting trees down realise how hard it is to grow them.

COMPASSION FOR ALL ANIMALS

Until he extends the circle of his compassion to all living things, man will not himself find peace.
Albert Schweitzer

The baby galah was waterlogged, all shivering and shaking, on the edge of the main road to Gresford when my husband saw him and stopped to pick him up. It had fallen out of a tree and could not fly back to the nest. The bird lady who lives at Telarah and helps with wildlife rescue took him off to have a bath, a delousing, and whatever else her rescue treatment involved, chatting all the while in a friendly voice 'What a lucky bird you are' and generally being delighted to receive another patient.

At a busy bushland corner near Bolwarra, I saw a large lizard, resembling a goanna, heading off across the road, so I pulled over in the hope that I could shuffle him back out of the traffic. I was beaten to it by a truckie who had also pulled over. 'Did you stop for the lizard, lady?' he called out. 'I told the silly bugger to get back under that bush,' then he waved and drove off.

When Abraham Lincoln was chided by friends for making them wait while he returned a fledgling to its nest he said, 'I could not have slept tonight if I had left that helpless little creature to perish on the ground.' He also wrote, 'I am in favour of animal rights as well as human rights. That is the way of the whole human being.'

Lincoln is not the only person to be criticised for helping animals. It is a familiar experience for many to be upbraided for wasting their time and money in such efforts, when there are so many humans who need help.

This sort of criticism is self-centred and short-sighted. All living creatures are connected, and to work with animals is to work at the heart of what we are ourselves. Compassion does not discriminate. It flows from the one source deep in our hearts. The man who stops to help a lizard is moved by the same impulse that leads to him helping another man. We are made of the same flesh and blood. It is our shared sufferings that make us equal.

Human superiority to the rest of nature – the belief that we are special and separate from all other beings – leads to callous indifference, and devastation of the world in its turn. The connection between how we treat animals and how we treat other people is inextricably linked. 'If you have men who will exclude any of God's creatures from the shelter of compassion and pity, you will have men who will deal likewise with their fellow men.' St Francis of Assisi (1181–1226).

The golden rule of treating others as you would like to be treated has a wider application than some might imagine. It is heartwarming to observe an act of kindness as simple as a gardener covering an earthworm with soil to protect it from the burning sun. Perhaps in witnessing the creature's plight, he had for a moment considered what it might be like if their positions had been reversed.

As a breeder of thoroughbreds I often find myself at horse sales. At one recently I listened in dismay to a stud groom as he tried to tell me in no uncertain terms that his horses were only machines. 'That is why they are sold to the knackery when their productive days are over, that's all they're good for.'

It would have been easy to refute such a patently ignorant remark. What he meant to say, and in his enthusiasm to shock me had got himself muddled, was that horses are commodities. With this I could have had no argument. Like cars and refrigerators they are bought and sold, but they are no more machines than the slaves of last century, and perhaps one day they will cease to be commodities as well.

It is people like that stud groom who always make me feel anxious when our yearlings head off to the sales. I fear they may not live out their lives cared for and content. Apart from that, I wonder about the man himself, his hardness of heart. Perhaps in his ignorance he thinks it manly to boast about his power over the lives of so-called lesser creatures.

At the same sales I watched two men trying to get a colt to board a transport float near the stable where my horses were housed. The nervous young animal kicked and would not move up the ramp, and the more he hesitated the angrier the men became, hitting him across the rump with a long stick, which merely made the animal more fearful, and things worse. If only they had stopped for a moment and put themselves in the horse's position, they might have solved the problem in a quieter, simpler way. Their lack of empathy with the horse made us bystanders increasingly upset, and one of the group, a horse buyer, walked off saying she couldn't bear to watch any longer.

It is with people like her – the trainers and breeders who exhibit time and again their devotion, not only to their horses but other animals as well, the gentle truckie who cares enough to stop for a lizard, the lady who cares for birds and countless others – that I see hope. Perhaps one day there will be enough people of this sort, setting examples of loving kindness that does not discriminate, confronting cruelty where they find it, so that in time attitudes towards other animals may change. I say other animals just as a reminder that, for all our sterile offices and concrete towers, which disconnect us from the world of nature, and our self-conceit and pretensions to be different, that is, after all, what we are too.

Devonshire Tea for Afternoon Visitors

This recipe was inspired by one given to me by my friend Stephen.
Until then I had always made scones by the usual method of rubbing
butter into the flour. I really liked the idea of substituting cream,
because somehow it seemed easier and quicker, so I altered his recipe
to suit myself but am grateful for yet another wonderful idea.
Makes about 12 scones

350 g (12 oz) self-raising flour
25 g (1 oz) castor sugar
½ teaspoon salt
2 large eggs, beaten
300 ml (10 fl oz) cream

▶ Preheat oven to 240°C (475°F).
▶ Sift the flour into a bowl with salt and sugar. Combine the egg and
cream and fork into the flour mixture. If it is too dry, add some water
to the cream jar, and use this liquid to finish making the scone dough.
▶ Pat to a round, 2 cm (1 in) high. Cut out scones and glaze with
some of the water/cream mix. Put on tray and bake for approximately
10 minutes.
▶ Serve immediately with strawberry jam and fresh thick or whipped
cream.

Variation For herb and cheese scones, add ¼ cup (4 tablespoons)
mixed chopped fresh parsley, thyme and chives and ½ cup
(50 g/2 oz) grated gruyère or another tasty cheese.

Pear Custard Tart

Serves 8

8 pears, halved, cored and peeled
120 g (4 oz) brown sugar
1 quantity sweet shortcrust pastry (see opposite)
1 x 28 cm (11 in) tart dish
300 ml (10 fl oz) cream
1 egg plus 2 yolks
120 g (4 oz) castor sugar
cinnamon

▶ Put the pears in a deep pan, cover with water, add brown sugar, bring to the boil, then simmer until just tender (approximately 10–15 minutes).
▶ Preheat oven to 200°C (400°F). Whisk the egg, yolks and castor sugar together, then stir in the cream.
▶ Line the tart dish with the pastry. Arrange the pear halves, round side up, in the uncooked pastry shell. Pour the cream mixture over and then sprinkle cinnamon on top.
▶ Bake in oven for 40–45 minutes, or until done.
▶ When cool dust with icing sugar to serve. Accompany with cream.

Variation You can substitute apples if preferred.

250 g (9 oz) plain flour, sifted
50 g (2 oz) almond meal
50 g (2 oz) icing sugar
150 g (5 oz) butter
1 egg

BY MACHINE

Put the sifted flour, almond meal and icing sugar together into the bowl of a food processor. Next add the butter in small pieces and combine with an on/off movement until the mixture resembles breadcrumbs. Work in the egg. The mixture should be nice and smooth – if not add a little water. Chill for half an hour before rolling.

BY HAND

Put the sifted flour, almond meal and icing sugar in a mound on your bench. Cut the butter into small pieces and work into these dry ingredients until the mixture resembles breadcrumbs. Work in the egg last of all. Chill for half an hour before rolling.

Serves 8

1 quantity puff pastry (see recipe page 66)
5 eggs
zest of 2 lemons
100 g (3½ oz) castor sugar
150 ml (5 fl oz) lemon juice
300 ml (10 fl oz) cream

▶ Line a deep tart tin with the rolled pastry. I use a large deep pie dish. A spring-form pan can be used – so that after the tart is cooked and cooled it can easily be taken out of to serve – but because the pan's sides are straight, and to prevent the pastry sliding down into one unusable mass at the bottom, it is necessary to roll the pastry a good deal wider than usual, then let it drape well over the sides of the tin. The excess pastry can be cut off later when the tart is cooked.
▶ Prick the pastry base well all over with a fork. Press aluminium foil to cover the pastry and fill to the brim with dried beans or rice. This keeps the pastry in place and ensures you end up with the desired shape to fill.
▶ Bake at 190°C (375°F) until the pastry has cooked into its shape, then remove the foil and continue cooking until the pastry case is nicely browned.
▶ In the meantime prepare the filling. Whisk the eggs well with the zest. Dissolve the sugar in the juice and stir into the eggs. Warm the cream almost to boiling, and stir in gradually. Pour the filling into the case and bake again for approximately 30 minutes, until set. Serve cold.

Fine Apple Tart

INGREDIENTS PER PERSON
puff pastry (see recipe page 66) leftovers will do
1 Granny Smith apple
castor sugar
unsalted butter

▶ Roll out the pastry as thinly as you can and drape it over a baking tray. Use a bread and butter plate: trace around its outside and cut out a circle of pastry. Prick all over very well with a fork. Repeat this for as many tarts as you wish to make. If you don't wish to bake them straight away, pile them like crepes onto a plate with plastic film between each one. Chill to firm and to make handling easier.
▶ Preheat oven to 190°C (375°F). Cut the apple in half from top to bottom, then peel, core and slice very thinly acrossways. Arrange the slices in overlapping circles on top of the pastry, finishing in the centre of each tart. Sprinkle liberally with sugar and dot just as liberally with butter. Bake in oven until the sugar caramelises, the apples are golden and the pastry crisp – approximately 15–20 minutes. If the apples are lacking a little colour, put the tarts under a very hot grill for a few seconds right at the end. Serve with vanilla ice cream.

April

I SPENT much of this April in England, touring the countryside, staying at comfortable country hotels, eating far too much, and visiting some wonderful gardens.

James and Amanda were left with lists of instructions, the most important of which was to 'get the seeds in'. And so they did. Packet after packet of poppy seeds were sown according to the 'barely scratch them in' method, and hundreds, if not thousands, of tiny plants were well on their way by the time I arrived home.

It was early spring in the English gardens, perhaps too early, but I won't complain, for if taken I would be happy to look at a garden under snow if necessary. The gardens I was most interested in were Christopher Lloyd's Great Dixter near Rye, and Rosemary Verey's Barnsley House at Barnsley in the Cotswolds. I felt at home in each, but my eye could easily pick the garden which belonged to the woman.

My diary notes read: Great Dixter – 'wild, self-sown plants growing in the cracks of steps and paths. Very homely and full of colour, mainly at this time of year from groupings of tulips. I am particularly taken by the area of wild grasses that one passes through on arriving. The topiary is quite mad. There is a distinctive personality at work here and I like its lack of formality.'

Barnsley House – 'A truly charming garden, again with lots of colour, tulips with masses of forget-me-nots. A happy lived-in look, the vegetable garden full of simple home-made trellises, and flowers amongst the vegetables. It is neat but also floppy. It has its formal elements with the temple and Gothic summerhouse, but it is not too big or in the slightest way pretentious.'

When I have been away in foreign places I always long to bring back the unfamiliar, but that's not easy, so for this trip packets of wallflower seeds in pretty shades of pink and lemon would have to suffice. The man at Customs gave them the okay, and the first thing I did when I arrived home was to 'scratch them in'.

I have visited many gardens over the years, some famous and others not in the least so. It amazes me what gardeners can achieve when they want to, even in the outback where a garden can survive from having precious water dippered onto it from the bath at the end of the day. It is also amazing what can be grown once a garden is under way. Microclimates produced by protective plantings mean that plants that could not have survived in the beginning when everything was harsh and bare are now not only possible, but can positively flourish. Delphiniums and foxgloves in my case, and lots more.

I am also surprised when gardens do not exist at all. When there is abundant sunshine, soil and water but no caring hands to plant. I have observed homes that never seem to emerge from the ugly, just-built bareness in which they began. I am convinced that there are people for whom the softening effects of trees and flowers are an alien concept. For them, a garden is not necessary for life, not like a television or truck. It is depressing to see homes dotted about the countryside with little more than a few straggly gums and a dead pot plant or two on the verandah. I know men who consider gardens a waste of time and money and effort, yet hulks of machinery and assorted vehicles necessary as life support. It is a brutish attitude, crushing to a more delicate spirit. When I see homes like this I dread to think what life must be like for those who live inside. Things seem to be so out of balance. The masculine element is too dominating, everything harsh and unsoftened by the feminine touch.

On the other hand there are women who – foolishly, in my opinion – think that the outdoor work has nothing to do with them. I have seen them with husbands reluctantly in tow measuring pergolas, making notes under instructions and looking thoroughly miserable while she of the well-kept nails and immaculate hair walks several paces ahead, all enthusiasm. Gardening is a funny business, and it can be a miserable business when partners are not on a wavelength.

There are few homes, from the simplest cottage to a palace, that do not benefit in a multitude of ways from the softening grace of a garden. Some people spend their time dreaming of paradise in heaven. I would rather try and create it here on earth.

PLANTING BULBS

It took me a long time to work out how I was going to grow bulbs in a garden so full of other things. Being visible for only part of the year, they seemed to take up precious space which I thought was best used by something more permanent.

But I love them too much to go without for want of a simple arrangement. Now what I do is to cluster about ten bulbs in one place – jonquils, daffodils, freesias, bluebells, it doesn't matter what they are – and plant a stick to mark the spot. Around these, a few weeks later, the seeds and seedlings are planted. These, being shallow-rooted and seasonal, don't interfere too much with the bulbs. Bulbs are perfectly happy growing underneath or very close to something that is shallow rooted, that will flower when the bulb has finished, and in turn will be pulled out or heavily cut back at that time when the bulbs will be wanting to push through again.

The jonquil 'Silver Chimes' grows in a secluded, semi-shaded spot under fragrant white buddleias. 'Erlicheer' is massed as a border at the edge of a low, brick retaining wall. Here in summer the seaside daisy, Erigeron, is a pretty show, all soft and frothy.

SEEDS

When putting in seeds, I rake the well-prepared soil to make it fine and even, scatter the seeds over and rake again. The seed packet is put on a stick as a marker, and everything watered. Seed beds need constant watering. I think one of the reasons people have trouble growing seeds is that they bury them too deeply.

Farm morning tea

Sometimes on Mondays, everyone who works on the farm congregates at my house for morning tea. Any small excuse will do – a birthday, a new staff member – just as long as there is plenty to eat, hot coffee, and the scones and rolls are hot from the oven.

Pumpkin Scones

1 tablespoon butter
100 g (3½ oz) sugar
1 cup (9 fl oz) mashed pumpkin, well drained
    (requires approximately 400 g/14 oz raw pumpkin)
1 egg, well beaten
350 g (12 oz) self-raising flour, sifted
a little milk, in case the mixture is too dry

▶ Preheat the oven to 240°C (475°F). Cream the butter and sugar together, add the pumpkin, the egg, and fork in the flour. Add milk if necessary.
▶ Pat dough gently to a round, 2 cm (1 in) high, cut the scones and bake for 10–15 minutes.

Ham Rolls

This recipe makes 3 long rolls, which cut up into approximately 24 little ones.

1 quantity puff pastry (see recipe page 66)
egg wash made from 1 egg mixed with 1 teaspoon water

FILLING
2 onions, chopped
a knob of butter
350 g (12½ oz) ham
1 tablespoon each parsley, thyme and sage, chopped and combined
freshly ground black pepper
2 eggs

▶ For filling, fry the onion in the butter until soft. Combine all filling ingredients in a food processor, adding the eggs at the end one at a time, making certain the mixture is not too wet. Purée smoothly, but not to a paste.
▶ Roll out the pastry into three strips approximately 16 cm (6½ in) wide and 60 cm (24 in) long. Roll the ham mixture by hand into three long sausage shapes and put each right down the centre of a pastry strip. Wrap the pastry over and seal with egg wash.
▶ Chill very well. Cut the rolls in half to make them easier to bake. Preheat oven to 220°C (430°F). Put rolls, seam-side down, onto a lightly floured baking tray, or one covered in baking paper. Brush with the remaining egg wash and bake until puffed and golden brown. This will take about 30 minutes. Slice into bite-size portions and serve hot.

500 g (1 lb) plain flour
500 g (1 lb) salted butter
1½ cups (14 fl oz) iced water
pinch of salt

▶ Let the butter sit at room temperature for a while to soften. It should be neither too soft or too hard.

▶ Sift the flour into a bowl and add the water, little by little, until you have worked it to a pliable dough (it will feel a bit like your earlobe). Rest dough in the refrigerator before continuing.

▶ Roll the dough out to a rectangular shape, approximately 60 x 20 cm (24 x 8 in). If you are using 250 g packs of butter, slice in two, lengthwise; cut 500 g packs into four. Place the four rectangles of butter, long edge to long edge, in one half of the rolled-out dough, leaving an edge of dough all the way around. Fold the empty half of dough over, and press the edges firmly together all the way around to enclose the butter in a parcel.

▶ Give the parcel a few whacks with the rolling pin to start to flatten it, then roll the pastry out away from you, flattening the butter inside as you do.

▶ Now fold the rolled-out pastry into three. Do this just as you would fold a business letter, with one edge inside. Make sure the edges are neatly aligned, and press down the outer edges firmly.

▶ Turn the pastry package so that the pressed edge is at your right, and the folded edge is at your left.

▶ Roll it out again, and fold as before, turn, press the edges together, roll out, press edges and turn. Mark the dough with two thumb prints (to indicate how many times you have turned it), wrap in aluminium foil, and rest in the refrigerator for 20 minutes before continuing.

▶ Repeat this folding and rolling procedure 4 more times. Rest in refrigerator for about 20 minutes before using. The length of resting time depends a bit on the weather – if it is very hot it will certainly need longer.

Note When rolling out the dough, sprinkle a little extra flour on the board and the rolling pin so that things don't stick. Brush off excess flour with a pastry brush. If little breaks in the dough should occur, patch and brush with a little flour.

200 g (7 oz) castor sugar
4 eggs, separated
1 boiled orange, pulverised in the blender
100 g (3½ oz) sweet orange marmalade
100 g (3½ oz) almond meal
2 tablespoons poppyseeds
150 g (5 oz) self-raising flour

ICING
150 g (5 oz) icing sugar
50 g (2 oz) soft butter
zest of 1 orange
orange juice

► Preheat oven to 190°C (375°F). Cream together the sugar and egg yolks. Add the orange pulp and marmalade. Fold in the almond meal, then the stiffened egg whites, poppyseeds, and the self-raising flour together.

► Put into a prepared cake tin (greased and floured and the base lined with baking paper), and bake in oven 1 hour or until done. Ice when cool.

► For icing, combine ingredients, adding sufficient orange juice to make a good icing consistency.

250 g (8 oz) raw sugar
4 eggs, separated
125 g (4 oz) soft butter
2 boiled oranges, pulverised in blender
200 g (7 oz) sweet orange marmalade
100 g (3½ oz) almond meal
150 g (5 oz) self-raising flour

ORANGE SYRUP
1½ cups (13½ fl oz) fresh orange juice
1½ cups (13½ oz) castor sugar

▶ Preheat oven to 190°C (375°F), but reduce the temperature by 10°C (25°F) if using a fan-forced oven. Cream the sugar and yolks, then add the butter, orange pulp, marmalade and almond meal. Beat egg whites until stiff, then fold them and the flour in together.

▶ Bake in a prepared pan for 1½ hours approximately. Serve with thick or whipped cream and orange syrup. This cake keeps very well.

▶ For the orange syrup, combine the sugar and juice, bring to the boil, then simmer, gently stirring until syrupy.

May

IT'S MAY. The early mist softens the landscape, hiding the hills till mid-morning. The garden looks drab and needs a good cutting back. Bearded iris are lifted, spent corms removed, the plants trimmed and replanted. There are so many after all this dividing that we end up heeling a lot in at the nursery. Lots of homeless baby iris and a lot of bare earth too, where seeds have been put in. The overall theme is brown. Brown earth, brown mulch, even the lawn is brown after the driest April for one hundred and fifty years.

Returning to the garden after three weeks in Europe is a shock too. It all seems so much rougher somehow, like the landscape, wild and untidy, and harsher too in the piercing light, lacking grace and softness. The newness of everything is irritating. I yearn for Cotswold stone walls and Gothic mansions, the picturesque and civilising effects that time brings.

It took a week for me to feel at home again and for satisfaction to creep back into my bones. I think it was something to do with the birds as much as recovering from jet lag. There is so much more life here. In the formal and not-so-formal gardens of France and Italy that I visited, I did not see or hear many birds. On the other hand, English gardens, with their hedges and more exuberant plantings, are full of little birds. But nothing can compare with the sight of fat kookaburras perched on the rose pergolas. I counted fifteen finch nests in the potato vine that smothers four large arches. Everywhere, without especially looking out for them, there are magpies, currawongs, egrets, ibis, ducks and wattlebirds, and it is not only the birds but the sound of frogs that warms my heart. I even begin to feel a fond attachment to the snake, and to make a virtue out of the wildness.

Over the week I've relearned what I always understood, that gardens mean different things to different people. The men who service the septic recycling tanks were overjoyed to find that we had removed the buddleias I had planted all around, in an attempt at some sort of disguise. 'Glad that jungle's gone,' said one. I thought, now there's something English gardens don't have to worry about, septic recycling tanks, or inground water tanks, which also need disguising, and ugly watering system pipes that must lie above ground, as we are forever stabbing them with forks the minute they are buried.

While I have trouble understanding what goes on in the minds of the septic recycling men – who don't seem to notice the garden at all and complain that they can't drive their truck across the lawn and through the hedges and park right alongside, it would be so much more convenient – I'm prepared to ignore them. We all have our biases. How many gardeners I know (mainly women) long to grow climbers and all sorts of vines up and over fences, walls and buildings, and equally as many husbands who moan and groan about roots in drains and clogged gutters and so on and so forth.

This is the dilemma faced by us all – practicality versus beautification. The problem with too much emphasis on practical things is that, like all things man-made, man-worried-about, it is anti-nature. The streamlined yard with its neat concrete paths, bare paling fences, trim lawns and equally trim plants, is not designed to encourage animals to live there. Variety is not only the source of life, but it is essential for life at all. Rainforests are complex healthy places, the opposite of bare and everything the same.

I am surprised too when I find gardeners busy killing every living thing they come across – scorpions, spiders, ants – just because they are there and have the potential to bite. It might have been extreme to carry the snails down to the creek to set them free when, as my mother used to say, they only marched right back over night and started chomping all over again. She killed hundreds when I wasn't looking, but I soon became more practical and bought snail bait, and also cabbage dust when caterpillars wiped out not just the cabbages, but the cleome as well. With the exception of flies and mosquitoes, everything else we leave alone, and I am still suspicious of anyone who can step on something as delicate, intricate and defenceless as a snail, without a pang.

There are many sorts of gardens and gardeners. My least favourite is the overly stylised minimalist sort of garden. Of course there is a place for them in busy lives, but what I really object to is a certain disdain on the part of minimalists, for the ornate, the cluttered and old-fashioned, as if their clean lines, with everything the same, are a sign of superior taste. I don't believe less is more. Less is less, and a sign of being hesitant for fear of making a mistake. Minimalism is restraint taken to an extreme. To me it lacks heart and personality, whether inside or outside the home. In a garden it literally lacks life. To be preoccupied with style is to be concerned more with the form than the substance of things, a pretty face rather than the deeper beauty of character. Such a sense of superiority is shallow and ultimately very boring.

It is also sad to see people slavishly following a fashion trend. If we are true to ourselves, I don't see how we can change the way we garden any more than we can change the way we write or paint. These things run deep. It is nothing to do with evolving and improving, but it is to do with how we see the world and the things that are close to the heart.

All gardens are beautiful in their own way, if tended by someone who cares about them. They reflect the owner's personality. Some talk about walking in their gardens to be calmed. I go to be cheered. Some people like clean, ordered, formal lines. Others like me must have flowers, and masses of them, in colourful, shaggy disarray.

East Gresford is the greater part of our neighbouring town, Gresford. It never looks to have a lot going on. In fact you would have to say it's very quiet, except when the annual show is on. At the supermarket I discovered some tulip bulbs for warmer climates, Monet's yellow and scarlet. I will pot these up and see if my luck with tulips changes.

Clusters of pots are something I was brought up with. Pots on steps, outside laundry doors, sunny verandahs and other nearby, easily watered places. Rosemary Verey had groups of pots in her garden at Barnsley. It was certainly my mother's habit and I wonder if it is something that women particularly like to do. It is certainly not the mark of a minimalist.

I'm at it again. I could hardly sleep last night for thinking about the new design we pegged out behind the studio, in another attempt to disguise the recycling tanks. I've ordered one hundred more *Juniperus chinensis* 'Spartan' for hedging, timber for two more rose pergolas and

James is digging out some of the flowering peach and plum trees that are suddenly in the way.

I've also been pulling out lots of dead daisies, and I'm beginning to think of them as annuals, the way they turn up their toes after one brief season. It seems no amount of good drainage is enough to cope with a couple of really wet days. I love them but they are so disappointing.

PLANTING

Now that the cool weather is here to stay we are planting in earnest. I am able to get in a hundred punnets in a day, as well as lots of seeds scattered inbetween. Amanda says that this is over the top and she's never seen anything like it, but I can only do this because the soil is ready, all nicely built up, easily forked through and free of weeds.

I don't place the punnets on the beds according to a plan – though I do have a few ideas worked out – but I like to leave them scattered about on paths so that I can wander about looking at them as I go along. Also I have packets of seeds to play with, orange Californian poppies, opium poppies, 'Fairy Wings' poppies and a white cottage poppy. These go in odd places amongst the other plants. For the Cottage Garden I have trays of cornflowers, plain deep blue and mixed colours, larkspurs, 'Pacific Giant' delphiniums, stocks (large doubles) and mixed foxgloves.

I work away in small patches at a time, a drift of blue cornflowers here, some Californian poppy seeds in a sweep above that, and the deep blue delphiniums further in. It is rather like building up a collage. I can work quickly because the soil is light and loose. The little plants can virtually be pushed in without any digging. At the end they are watered in by hand using a watering can and liquid fertiliser, a complete plant food or soil conditioner like Seasol. This gets their little roots off to a good start.

While planting the punnets and seeds I am also moving other things about, regrouping plants that have become isolated from their companions or that somehow look odd and out of place now. The garden is continually shifting.

One thing I do think is important is to mass like plants together for a show. To plant just one or two of anything is just not enough to make an impact. Better to plant seven of one thing closely together – not all scattered about so that they look lost or lonely. I also prefer drifts and circles, squiggles and sweeps, to rows of equally spaced plants looking like a council garden, all neat and orderly, but lacking heart.

Facing page: The old barn

May

Why I read stories

Clara (Clara Monroe in *The Last of the Mohicans*, Nathaniel
   Hawthorne)
Lizzie (Elizabeth Bennett in *Pride and Prejudice*, Jane Austen)
Dorothea (Dorothea Brook in *Middlemarch*, George Eliot)

I have three heroines, all characters from books that I love, imaginary
people whom I admire for one reason or another, identify with and try
to emulate – though not very well. I carry them around in my mind
like handy little sayings or proverbs, ready to refer to when things get
difficult. As a source of inspiration they are marvellous.

There they are when I feel myself being bullied, reminding me how
to put on a brave face, how to confront the terrifying. It is possible that
over time I have endowed them with attributes not given by their
authors, that I have become confused and made them an amalgam
of other people I know, real or fictional. Whatever the truth, Clara's
insightfulness into her own nature, her honesty and sheer physical
courage in the face of savagery, Lizzie's ironic outlook and defiant
stance towards the superficial and superior, and Dorothea's idealism
and lack of material aspirations, have helped me in one way or another
to cope with the people I have met and had to deal with over the years.

The things they have taught me are mostly to do with courage and
dignity. They are all wounded by life, suffer the pangs of grief,
embarrassment, rejection, despair. They weep and get angry, but
they do not give up easily or fall into passivity or become pitiful,
helpless victims.

They are all true to an inner longing for truth. They are reflective,
resourceful, life-loving, strong, determined and deeply passionate.
Above all they are courageous, and this I think is the most difficult of
all things to be. Our circumstances differ, but people remain much
the same. The Maguas, Lady Catherines and Casaubons are out there
today, still full of self conceit, and just as hard to deal with.

When I have to do something difficult, particularly when I have to
confront someone I don't like, deliver bad news, reject or disappoint
someone, I tremble and wish the ground would swallow me up. It's
just so much easier to run away from difficult situations, or to agree
with the other person's point of view. Particularly in a group situation,
it is so tempting to go along with everyone else rather than be true to
oneself and suffer possible rejection.

This is where my heroines help, for they remind me that pain of all
kinds, be it rejection, failure, even grief, can be transforming, or as we

say when laughing at all the day-to-day disappointments that seem without end, 'This is character building.'

So a very large part of why I read stories is to look for people to admire, people about whom I can say, 'I'd like to be like that'. I read in order to understand the struggle and inner turmoil of the human mind as it searches for a better life and to find such characters and such a quest I find myself continually reverting to the classical fiction of previous centuries.

It is through reading the very best literature, or watching the very best drama, that we are able to grasp the meaning of the natural virtues honoured by the ancient Greeks. Prudence, justice, fortitude and temperance are needed as much in our lives today as then. Unless one is fortunate in having excellent acquaintance, I know of no other way to learn the lessons so well.

FAVOURITE FOODS

There are two things I would find impossible to choose between on a menu – fish quenelles and liver pâté with toasted brioche. I simply adore them both. They are classic dishes, painstaking to make, and probably for that reason, the difficulty of choosing between them rarely presents itself. Then again, perhaps not many people feel the same way that I do, about this and other things beside.

There are two restaurants I know that make superb quenelles – Tour d'Argent in Paris and The Connaught Hotel, London. The liver is readily available overseas in the various forms of foie gras, but because I don't like the way foie gras is produced using methods of forcefeeding ducks and geese, I indulge my passion a little closer to home. Superb liver parfaits can be made with unfattened liver. In Sydney, the restaurants Banc and Merronys both have excellent versions from time to time.

Here are my recipes for these favourite dishes.

Fish Quenelles

Makes 16–20 quenelles

FISH STOCK

2 kg (5 lb) trimmings and bones of John Dory, whiting, sole or any other
   white-fleshed, delicate flavoured fish
1 large carrot
1 large onion
1 large leek (white part only)
3 or 4 parsley stalks
1 celery stalk
6 black peppercorns
500 ml (16 fl oz) dry white wine
1.5 litres (2½ pints) water

FISH MOUSSE

200 g (7 oz) scallops
330 g (12 oz) sole, whiting or red fish
1 egg
600 ml (1 pint) cream
pinch each salt and white pepper

CHOUX PASTRY

250 ml (8 fl oz) cold water
50 g (2 oz) unsalted butter
135 g (4½ oz) flour
pinch of salt
6 eggs

SAUCE

600 ml (1 pint) cream
100 g (3½ oz) grated gruyère cheese
½ teaspoon each white pepper and salt

▶ To make the stock, chop and wash the fish bones thoroughly. Wash and chop all the vegetables, and put with the fish bones and peppercorns into a stock pot. Cover everything with the cold water and wine and bring to the boil. Skim away the scum, and reduce to a gentle simmer for 20–25 minutes. Do not overcook the stock or it may become bitter. Strain through a conical sieve, pushing everything well down to extract every bit of juice and flavour. Rest for a few minutes and skim if necessary.

▶ To make the mousse, purée the scallops and fish together in a food processor. Put the purée into a bowl set over ice. Using a wooden spoon or spatula work in the egg first, then the cream, a little at a time. Pass the mixture through a sieve or mouli, then through muslin or some other fine kitchen cloth. These steps are essential in producing a fine, smooth texture. Season with salt and pepper. Test the flavour by poaching a little drop of mixture in a pan of simmering fish stock.

▶ To make the pastry, put the cold water and butter together in a saucepan and bring to the boil. Remove from the stove and stir in the flour and salt all at once, stirring briskly all the while. Return to the stove and cook gently while continuing to stir, until the mixture dries and leaves the sides of the pan. Remove from the stove once again and add the eggs one at a time, making sure that each egg is well incorporated before adding the next. The mixture will become smooth and shiny. Cool.

▶ Combine the fish mousse and choux pastry together thoroughly. Poach spoonfuls in the simmering fish stock. I use an oval ice-cream scoop to create a nice quenelle shape. Poach on both sides, for about 5 minutes per side. The mixture will swell. Remove with a slotted spoon and lay on a towel to drain. These can be kept in a dish in the refrigerator for one or two days until needed.

▶ To serve, combine all sauce ingredients, bring to the boil and then simmer until thick. Put two quenelles in individual gratin dishes and cover with the sauce. Warm through in the oven, then place under a hot grill to brown.

Variation Place quenelles on a bed of finely diced mushrooms, cooked in butter and finished with a little cream, pepper and salt, before covering with the sauce.

Liver Parfait

Serves 8–10

500 g (1 lb) fresh duck or chicken livers
  (these need to be very well trimmed so buy 750 g/1½ lb)
2 eggs
300 ml (10 fl oz) cream
2 teaspoons madeira
¼ teaspoon each salt and white pepper
125g (4 oz) butter, melted
500 ml (1 pint) or thereabouts, clarified chicken stock

▶ Preheat the oven to 180°C (350°F). Trim the livers very well of all threads and bits of gall. Wash, drain, and pat dry and purée in a food processor. Add the eggs one at a time, then the cream, madeira, salt and pepper, and last of all the melted butter.

▶ Pass this mixture through a fine sieve and then through double layers of muslin – or other fine kitchen cloth – to remove all the unwanted specks. Butter a 26 cm (10 in) oven dish and pour the mixture in. Bake for 12 minutes, until just firm, so that the inside stays pink.

▶ Chill well, and when absolutely cold, pour the clarified stock over and chill again so that the stock sets to a jelly.

▶ To serve, roll jellied liver into quenelle shapes, using a spoon dipped in hot water. Serve 1 or 2 rolls per person, and accompany with a slice of toasted brioche (see recipe on page 80). You can also accompany the liver with a spoonful of fig jam (see my mother's recipe in August, page 113).

Brioche

20 g (¾ oz) fresh yeast
4 tablespoons warm water
500 g (1 lb) flour
60 g (2 oz) castor sugar
6 eggs
300 g (11 oz) unsalted butter, softened
a little egg wash (1 yolk mixed with a teaspoon of water)

▶ Mix the yeast with warm water until pasty. Sift the flour into a mixing bowl or food processor bowl with dough hook attached. Add the sugar and stir in the yeast mixture. Now add the eggs one at a time. Add the butter bit by bit as you continue to mix, and the dough begins to form an elastic ball. At a slow speed it will take about 10–15 minutes for the desired elasticity to be reached.

▶ Put the dough in a well-greased loaf tin, and set to rise in a warm place. This will take 1–2 hours. To begin with, the dough will half fill the tin. When risen it will have doubled in bulk.

▶ When the dough is ready, preheat the oven to 240°C (475°F), then brush the top of the loaf with egg wash and bake in the hot oven for 10 minutes; then turn oven right down to 180°C (350°F) for a further 30 minutes. Test with a skewer. When inserted right in the centre of the loaf for a few seconds, it should come out clean and hot to touch. When done, turn loaf out on a wire rack to cool.

I cannot think about favourite food and leave out quinces, just stewed, with cream.

They can be peeled, cored, and sliced first, covered with water, with about a cup of sugar for every six quinces, brought to the boil, then simmered until tender. Or you can stew them whole, with the water and sugar, until tender, cool, peel and slice afterwards.

I prefer the first method, as I have more control over seeing when they are just right, despite the arduousness of peeling something like a rock.

Curried Pumpkin Soup

In May pumpkins growing on the creek bank begin to ripen.
Serves 4–5

2 tablespoons butter
2 large onions, peeled and sliced
1 medium potato, peeled, washed and sliced
1 kg (2 lb) peeled, seeded and chopped pumpkin
2 sprigs parsley
2 tablespoons curry powder
black pepper and salt to taste
250 ml (9 fl oz) milk
2 teaspoons fennel seeds
60 ml (2½ fl oz) sour cream

▶ Melt the butter in a pot and fry the onion until soft. Add the potato
and pumpkin, parsley, curry powder and salt and pepper, just cover
with water, bring to the boil, then simmer until everything is very well
cooked.
▶ Put into a blender, blend and add the milk to thin. At the end stir
in the fennel seeds and sour cream and adjust the seasoning.

Field Mushroom and Garden Herb Soup

Mushrooms are also plentiful this month after autumn rains.
Serves 4

1 large onion, peeled and chopped
1 clove garlic, peeled and chopped
1 tablespoon butter
500 g (1 lb) mushrooms
1 large potato, peeled, washed and chopped
handful of fresh basil leaves and parsley, or some oregano, roughly chopped
1 teaspoon salt
a good grinding of black pepper
125 ml (5 fl oz) red wine
375 ml (15 fl oz) water
500 ml (scant pint) milk
250 ml (9 fl oz) sour cream

▶ Gently fry the onion and garlic in the butter until soft. Add the mushrooms, potato and herbs, the salt and pepper, then the red wine and boil to reduce by more than half. Add the water and simmer until the potato is tender. Add the milk towards the end and boil for a further couple of minutes. Whisk in the sour cream. Purée everything smooth using a blender. Adjust the seasoning if necessary.

June

A PELICAN wheels high over the garden, checking us out. Dry leaves crackle underfoot in the grass. The Powton leaves are enormous, like elephant's ears, and the bare branches covered in buds are beautiful against the greying sky.

In the Bright Border all the poppy seeds are up – tulip poppies, 'Lady Bird', 'Shirley', 'Orange Chiffon', Iceland poppies and white cottage. So too are the strawflowers, poached-egg plant – self-sown from last year – and godetia. There are delphiniums everywhere. Amanda says that you can never have too many delphiniums. I remind her of Russell Page's precept that plants should have their own particular stage on which to show off their charms, and that as our delphiniums are everywhere, I think he'd say they're overacting.

The night closes in early these days, time for wood fires and hot puddings. At Torryburn we sleep deeper and eat more. Usually after breakfast I inspect the garden to see if there are any changes – since yesterday. These mornings I spend a lot of time writing or painting in the studio. Weeding does not come until later in the day. Even in winter this job is neverending, but I find it soothing in its mindless, repetitive way. Sometimes I feel it's all I'm good for.

It's still and grey, not a breath of wind. Butterflies dance over the ageratum, attracted to the blue flowers. More seeds are up, masses of love-in-the-mist, and daffodils poking through them. The first daffodil is in bloom and all manner of other bulbs that I'd forgotten about, mainly snowflakes and jonquils. I'm always surprised at the number that survive being chopped up or cast into the hot sun.

The frosts make us go looking for protective hessian sacks. From now on the heliotropes and nasturtiums will be tucked up snugly every night. It will not absolutely prevent frostbite, but it might stop total annihilation.

The pelican came back. I woke to see him – or is it her? – swimming like a bright-eyed boat up and down the front dam. After another early morning shower the sky is pale blue between grey clouds. I get a lot of pleasure out of these wet wintry days for they can be spent indoors with a clear conscience. But not Mondays.

Neither gale-force winds or this ongoing rain can stop us gardening on Mondays. All mud and plastic, unable to hear a thing underneath plastic hoods, we shovel mushroom compost on top of the glug and plant in drifts the remaining seedlings of white foxgloves. At last we are in the front garden. Here a wild strawberry I once bought at a nursery thinking it a pretty thing has spread and entangled itself everywhere, becoming our worst weed.

A perfect pair of weeping mulberries have been planted either side of the steps, in the centre of beds of equal size and shape. The beds are edged with bidens and the trees underplanted with forget-me-nots, wallflowers and gaillardias. Bidens is a wonderful plant, with its frothy, fern-like foliage and cheery yellow star-shaped flowers. It is easily propagated from cuttings. It surprises me to hear that bidens does not sell very well at the local nursery. I believe it is something to do with people not wanting yellow in the garden. This is astonishing given how a touch of yellow will make the blues and pinks really sing. That is also true when it comes to painting flowers in watercolour.

I would not be without the yellows and oranges, particularly in combination with purple. For instance, in the Vegetable Garden, the deep purple leaves of the giant mustard are surrounded by the bright yellow and orange calendulas, while purple cabbages sit alongside soft yellowy-green mignonettes. In the summer Cottage Garden, Swane's apricot cottage rose 'Devon' is a sight to behold surrounded by the deepest blue salvia, a sea of nasturtiums that want to go everywhere, bright orange geums and the yellow bidens. Pineapple lilies push through this mixture, and as a backdrop, giving height and more vivid colour, are the weeping 'Dorothy Perkins', wondrous 'Crepuscule' climbing on a pillar and a towering purple buddleia.

James has decided that I need a special flower garden just for picking. This is because I am sometimes loath to disturb a pretty sight and prefer to see the blooms in the garden than in a vase. In the vegetable garden beside the creek, that is his own special province, there are zucchinis, chillies and capsicums surrounded by delphiniums, larkspurs, cornflowers and ranunculus. I'm told they must be picked.

The leaves of the baby Chinese tallow woods in the front park are every shade from yellow to red. The liquidambars are purple, and gradually dropping. The pin oaks are only ever brown.

Last night I was walking the dogs along the creek. I enjoy the peace of these few relaxed snake-free months. Suddenly I looked up through the bare branches of the willows as the sky and the surrounding hills turned pink.

I saw a fox the other day, so the hens' yard is checked thoroughly, just in case there are holes in the netting.

Turning fifty

This month, this year, and very much to my surprise, I turned fifty, wondered how this was possible, and began to reflect on the barely noticed passing of time, stamped as it is for all the world to see across our brows, in ways we are scarcely aware of.

I thought I would always be the same. Always the heroine of my own particular sort of dream, full of wonder at a not-as-yet determined future, and I simply can't believe it. I'm too young to be fifty.

Yet I would not be young again either, all timidity and uncertainty. I don't have to put up with people I don't like anymore, nor do I try to impress. I'm much more able to speak my mind these days, but the candour is tempered with increased tolerance and patience. I'm less inclined to try and prove a point, particularly if I feel the other person is fixed in their opinion anyway. Also I don't worry quite as much as I once did about what other people think of me, and will rise up like a fury in the face of arrogance or rudeness, or if I see someone being treated unfairly.

This is because, for me, age brings confidence and a greater feeling of acceptance of oneself, and this in turn brings power. The best thing about being fifty is at last being able to be oneself. Murmurings that have been locked up deep inside are allowed to pop out now. We try so hard to be dignified when young, and now that we are older, by

some strange twist, we are able more truly to acknowledge the child within, and be ourselves.

The problem seems to be that fifty sounds old, and in the minds of some marks the beginning of a sort of grey solemnity, all stiff and conservative, lacking the spark of youthful vigour and enthusiasm.

Being fifty I still want to run and jump, climb trees, dance and sing. It's not time to sit in a bower and watch the bees and accept that all the spicy bits of life's experiences belong to the past. Being fifty, one still likes to be fancied.

What I think is over is a lot of the struggling to get on. The groundwork of life is done, and being older does bring some relief and the freedom to do different things. Men become less coy as well, more like real people, real friends, respectful and less inclined to headpat – definitely less frightened. It is as if a cloud of anxiety that hangs over younger relationships lifts as we become stronger and more serene.

The older we get the more conscious of death we become, and this increased awareness makes us live more in the present moment and less in fretful longing for the future. As we weather the pains of personal sorrows, we do get a little tougher and a sort of wisdom grows.

One thing I have learned is that timidity never got anyone anywhere. Whether it's a class of unruly children, a cranky husband, or a growling dog – always stick up for yourself, I say. Never let the other side know you're frightened. I don't mean not to admit when you're wrong. That's different. That is straight and honest and honorable, for there's nothing worse than trying to shift the blame, never being the one at fault. But don't give in for the sake of peace. How many women do, and in the end it never gets them anywhere, only deeper inside an interminable prison. Better to struggle and clash and shake the foundations. Stick up for yourself, be tough, even when you think love is at stake – for it never is.

At fifty I'm never bored or unable to wait for a certain calendar event. Neither am I easily knocked sideways when things don't quite turn out as I would have liked. The best part is the incredible freedom and the sense that most, if not all, things are still possible, and whatever is not possible is not worth worrying about.

Lemon Delicious

Serves 3–4

50 g (2 oz) butter
200 g (7 oz) castor sugar
3 eggs, separated
85 g (3 oz) self-raising flour
500 ml (scant pint) milk, or 250 ml (9 fl oz) milk and 250 ml (9 fl oz) cream
grated rind and juice of 1 lemon (about 50 ml/2 fl oz juice)

▶ Preheat oven to 190°C (375°F).
▶ Cream the butter and sugar together and then the egg yolks. Stir in the flour, the lemon juice and rind, and gradually the milk and cream. Whisk the egg whites until stiff and fold into the mixture.
▶ Put the mixture into a deep, buttered soufflé dish and bake for 45 minutes. Serve straight from the oven with thick cream.

Variation Substitute the pulp of 2 passionfruit for the lemon.

Sticky Date Pudding with Butterscotch Sauce

Serves 8–10

400 g (14 oz) pitted dates, chopped
250 ml (9 fl oz) boiling water
1½ teaspoons bicarbonate of soda
50 g (2 oz) butter
250 g (9 oz) brown sugar
2 large eggs
250 g (9 oz) self-raising flour

SAUCE
340 g (12 oz) brown sugar
250 ml (9 fl oz) water
100 g (3½ oz) butter
600 ml (1 pint) cream

► Soak the dates in the boiling water, stir in the bicarbonate of soda and set aside. Preheat the oven to 180°C (350°F).

► Cream the butter and sugar. Add the well-beaten eggs. Fold in the flour and the date mixture. Pour into a buttered oven dish – about 21 x 21 x 5 cm (8½ x 8½ x 2 in) – and bake for about 1½ hours (or until an inserted skewer comes out hot and clean.) Small individual puddings can be made. These will take approximately 30 minutes to cook

► For the sauce, put the sugar and water together in a pot and boil to reduce by half, then add the butter, stirring until melted, then the cream, and boil again to reduce to a thickened sauce consistency – you will notice the bubbles becoming large at this point. Pour the hot sauce over each individual serving, with thick or whipped cream on the side.

Bread and Butter Pudding

Serves 3

50 g (2 oz) sultanas
2 large slices white bread, crusts removed
butter
marmalade
2 eggs plus 1 yolk
75 g (3 oz) castor sugar
½ teaspoon vanilla essence
250 ml (9 fl oz) cream

To make this pudding I use an old-fashioned ovenproof glass oval dish that holds about a litre (2 pints) liquid.

▶ Preheat oven to 190°C (375°F). Butter the dish and sprinkle half the sultanas over the bottom. Spread the bread with butter and marmalade (not too much) and slice diagonally into quarters. Layer the bread butter-side up in the dish.

▶ Whisk the eggs, sugar, vanilla and cream together and pour over the bread. Sprinkle the remaining sultanas on top and bake for 45–50 minutes or until set. Serve hot accompanied with cream – but it's also nice cold, and can be reheated.

July

I'VE BEEN losing heart again. Everything seems to be standing still, bleak and unpromising. So I have just been sitting watching the birds instead of weeding. At dusk flocks of galahs, ducks in pairs and ibis occupy the front park. The black coots are everywhere, comical looking with their big feet and long, ungainly red legs. I saw one trying to balance on top of the barn, slipping and sliding until it gave up and flew off, embarrassed. It's the coots that cry out at night, a piercing shriek, rather as if they are being strangled.

Wattles are coming into flower, lots of Cootamundras in amongst the young gums splash brightest yellow into the green landscape. I shall pick bunches for the house without worrying about anyone's hayfever and getting into trouble for bringing that damned stuff inside. The smell is another childhood memory.

James and David are doggedly pruning trees, the entire grove of Chinese poplars, the orchard, the flowering plums, cherries and crabapples under which I have been trying to establish a wild meadow of bulbs. Jonquils are struggling through the thick grass. There are daffodils and snowflakes as well, but I'm not sure the idea is working very well – not with kikuyu. Perhaps when this season's flowering is finished we will dig them up and rethink what can be done. Wild areas of uncut grasses work well if the mixture is not dominated by one thing or another, and that's the trouble with mine and why it just looks a mess.

The new roses are all in, including the three my father gave me for my birthday, 'Papa Meilland', 'Karen Blixen' and 'Aotearoa', planted together so that in years to come I can look at them and remember him. The new circular rose garden at the front is filled with shades of yellow. We have divided and planted catmint at its edge. This rose–catmint combination is a recurring theme, the soft blue and silvery grey forming a perfect border for the gnarled angular rose bushes. 'New Dawn' and 'Albertine' are planted at the base of the new pergolas. James had these built in a flash after we decided that the border walk needed added length and perspective. The walk, known to all of us as 'the Mr Darcy walk', was dug and planted while in weekly raptures over the television serialisation of *Pride and Prejudice,* and thus named in hope that Mr Darcy lookalikes may wander along and surprise us at our gardening. Apart from that, the kookaburras love having extra vantage posts. They sit for ages concentrating on some unfortunate wriggling thing below, then swoop, gobble, back to the lookout, all fat and fluffed up.

Some of the days now are the most perfect of the year. We wake to frost-whitened paddocks and mist rising from the low country. Only a few puffy clouds in a pale blue sky, everything still and basking. After lunch on such a day, I lie on the grass and soak in the sun, watching ants clambering through the stalks, listening to the frogs down in the creek and all sorts of birds in the garden, particularly the wrens and finches. They don't seem to mind whether plants are native or not. The tiny ones in particular make nests in anything, weeping roses, plumbago, daisies, dwarf conifer. In the evening rosellas come in to give the lawns a good pecking over.

Earlier this year the calicivirus was released in our area and we enjoyed a few rabbit-free months. Now they are back, digging up the little trees to eat the roots, sometimes snapping the tops off completely and ringbarking the bigger ones. Once more we have to put chicken-wire guards around everything vulnerable – that includes the baby vegetables.

Thinking about the vegetables brings me to the subject of manure and manure gathering which, like picking mushrooms, is a pleasant enough way to spend a few hours. Frank is the stud teaser, a short, gingery sort of horse, friendly and good at his job. He came to us with the formidable reputation of being the best teaser in Australia, a job which involves a lot of association but not actual contact with mares. The men all feel sorry for Frank, particularly at the end of a busy season, but I'm not impressed. I feel sorrier for the mares, who don't seem to get much of a say in things.

I do, however, like the neat little piles of manure, a male habit, that Frank leaves behind for me. Frank manure is wonderful for the roses

One of the hills around Gresford

and the vegetables. Some gets put into a large lidded bin that is then topped up with water and kept somewhere handy with a dipper. It makes a perfect supply of liquid fertiliser. The only trouble is finding somewhere inconspicuous for the drum which, like a lot of practical necessities, is unsightly.

Clotheslines are another problem. I went without one for years while deliberating how to combine the drying of clothes with beauty. In the end I gave in to the Hills hoist principle of the big umbrella, as it would fit neatly into a corner, but made my own using a post of treated pine, thin rods strung with wire, and stuck a carved wooden goat's head on top.

Apart from manure, my other great garden fetish is mushroom compost, which is delivered in truckloads. Down behind the nursery are three large corrugated iron bins, and into these goes the compost, our stable straw full of urine and manure, and an all-purpose loamy soil. The garden needs constant building up, using compost, manure, leaf litter – it doesn't much matter what it is, onto the garden it goes.

This morning I woke to the terrible news that a fox had taken all my fowls. James was as nonplussed as I was, as he had secured the yard along Fort Knox guidelines. I feel sad that I was not able to better protect them, so gentle and defenceless as they were. And I'll miss them too – all individual characters, particularly Bruce the bantam rooster.

Foxes are everywhere. I see them at dusk around the creek, and wonder if the changes in the rabbit population are somehow related. I like foxes and feel sympathy for them too – victims of the hunt, villains of the fairy tale. Where I live in Sydney near Lane Cove, a fox used to appear at my back door every night, looking for dinner. It ate from my hand with the daintiness of a cat, and had a particular liking for roast chicken. Now I must consider shooting them.

The rest of the day was not without its pleasures. I managed to convince everyone that an alteration to the fencing behind the big front dam would be more pleasing to the eye if we eliminated the 'dog-leg'. It would not take too much land from the adjoining horse paddock and would give me more space for tree planting which, in turn, some time in the future, would create marvellous reflections in the water.

It's funny how you exist for years with something, accepting the way it is, then suddenly recognise that it desperately needs alteration. Fortunately for me – or them – everyone agreed, particularly David, who as Stud Master is quite rightly somewhat loath to cede more land to gardens. We already have far more than is considered normal. But perhaps he is not a normal Stud Master; having once grown roses commercially, he seems a little more appreciative than most to floral beauty. He even helped out last Monday with our winter pruning, in a very organised, neat and tidy manner, his clippings placed on a hessian sack as he went along. I'm of the school that throws them over the shoulder and picks up later.

The local nurseryman at East Gresford assures me that even though deciduous, the witch hazel is wonderful for screening. I always listen to his advice because he is growing things just down the road in the same climatic conditions. He arrived within an hour of my phoning with all the trees – a mixture of Norfolk pines and the witch hazel – so it was time to start pulling fences down and relocating them, digging holes and mowing and poisoning a circle of grass at each tree site ready for planting. The Norfolks are about three metres high and will need staking immediately as they appear top-heavy and August winds are just around the corner.

Much of today was spent planning and placing orders. For the time that remained we pruned more roses, this time in the Walled Garden, scrubbing some with warm soapy water to remove white scale. Wheelbarrow loads of manure were bucketed around, particularly where young plants are struggling to get a go on.

James planted the Persian silk tree in the front garden in a position that was obviously requiring a tree with height. He also relocated a struggling Japanese maple overwhelmed by a neighbouring Chinese elm, to the front park. Amanda insists that this now empty spot is crying out for a fountain of some kind. I'll think about it.

Monday is our special gardening day for it is the day we all work together, James, David, Amanda and me, and it is the only day Amanda is here.

She is much more than a talented horticulturalist. She is an elf, bobbing about in a straw hat, an enthusiast and a friend who loves the garden and spurs me on when I give signs of drooping. She too began her life as a music teacher, but now it's plants, and she knows far more about them than I do.

I still like to think I've taught her a thing or two, odd things, like not being timid when it comes to knocking seedlings out of their punnets, and merely scratching seeds into the ground, planting odd numbers in drifts, and using bright colours together. She's got a good eye for colour but her preferences were for a time, I think, of the softer kind. She often draws my attention to something I've missed and she considers pretty, like the silvery combinations of white jonquils clustered under a group of fragrant white buddleias. While I observe the overall, it's Amanda who spies the detail. While there are numerous Amanda-ish things happening in every corner of the garden, I must make particular note of the fact that it was she who first started putting violas into the herb garden.

We start at 8 a.m. or earlier, but it takes a while to warm up. First find some clean gardening gloves, then collect a wheelbarrow, fork, spade and secateurs, all usually needed over the course of a day. Now decide which area to work in.

Morning tea is at ten, lunch at one, and we stop around four. Neither rain, the worst winds of August or a summer 40°C blast stops Monday from happening. That's not just because the garden needs us, but because we need each other. There can be little that is more enjoyable than a tête-à-tête with people of similar tastes, while weeding or planting.

PRUNING ROSES

Late July is rose pruning time. This is because there will be more frosts ahead, and it is better to put off the pruning than to have new growth on the roses blackened off.

It is not a difficult job once you stop being frightened about it and realise that it is most unlikely that you will hurt the plants, even if you use a chain saw. Just get stuck in.

Secateurs to the gardener are like knives to the cook. They are respected and kept in good order. It always makes a job easier if the tools used are of the best quality. Our secateurs and pruning saws are kept clean and sharp, and when in use are dipped in diluted bleach, as we move from bush to bush, to help prevent disease spreading.

Cut on the slant above a bud pointing outwards, making sure there are no coathangers – little bits left at an angle that should be cut off – and the plant is left with only clean major growth, the size of the bush being reduced by about a third or even more.

Some roses are left completely alone. These are the climbers, the banksias, 'Dorothy Perkins' and 'Seneca Alba', which flower on one-year-old wood, and are pruned after flowering, or only if they become too wild and a nuisance.

PUB FOOD

One of the most disappointing aspects of living in this part of the country is the scarcity of good eating places. Pubs are an example of what I mean. Good pub food is great. One of the things I enjoy most when touring around Great Britain is happening upon an old-fashioned pub for lunch. I don't mean the commercialised chain variety with their formulas of mediocrity, but family-run places where good home cooking still thrives. Menus that are too extensive, that cater to the palate of the junk-food addict, where nothing is freshly made, where everything comes out of a giant freezer, is microwaved and then fried – and even the chips, despite all the frying practice, are terrible – is eating out at its worst. The pity is that to do it better is just so easy with a smaller menu, fresh ingredients, and homely dishes like shepherd's pie, fish cakes and roast dinners on Sunday.

Welsh Rarebit

Serves 4

150 g (5 oz) grated cheddar cheese
1 large tablespoon horseradish cream
1 large tablespoon Dijon mustard
black pepper
1 teaspoon salt
cream
4 slices bread, crusts removed

▶ Put the bread to one side and mix all the other ingredients together with enough cream to make a spreading consistency.
▶ Toast the underside of the bread, then spread the other side with the topping and grill until bubbling and golden brown. Serve alone or with dressed greens and bacon rashers.

Shepherd's Pie

Serves 6

There's more than one way to cook this popular family dish. My friend Barbara only uses cooked lamb, onions and beef stock under the potato crust. Very English. My brother Mark would be generous with garlic and tomato. I never make it the same way twice, and often clean out the pantry of leftover sauces and relishes when I do. So the following recipe is merely a suggestion.

500 g (generous lb) cooked lamb (leftovers from a leg, for example)
250 g (9 oz) onion, chopped and fried
250 ml (9 fl oz) fresh tomato purée with basil leaves
250 ml (9 fl oz) leftover gravy (or rich veal stock, see recipe page 44)
2 tablespoons Worcestershire sauce
2 teaspoons salt (or to taste)
mashed potatoes
grated tasty cheese

▶ Preheat oven to 200°C (400°F). Set aside the potato and cheese and put everything else into a blender and combine until smooth. Put into the bottom of a pie dish, cover with the mashed potatoes, sprinkle cheese over and bake until bubbly and brown. This recipe can be made in individual ramekins.

Steak and Kidney Pie

Serves 3

2 large onions, peeled and chopped
3 large sprigs parsley
2 tablespoons butter
500 g (generous lb) round steak, cubed
2 lamb kidneys, chopped
black pepper
salt
3 tablespoons plain flour
250 ml (9 fl oz) red wine
500 ml (scant pint) beef stock
3 tablespoons Worcestershire sauce
½ quantity puff pastry (see recipe page 66)

▶ Gently fry the onion and parsley in the butter in the bottom of a heavy, non-stick lidded pot. When soft add the beef and kidney, give a good grinding of black pepper, and a couple of pinches of salt, and brown. Sprinkle the flour over and stir in. Add the red wine, bring to the boil, then add the beef stock and Worcestershire sauce. Bring back to the boil, then cook very gently with the lid on for about 1½ hours, or until the meat is tender. Taste and adjust the seasoning if necessary. Take off the lid and bring back to a high heat to reduce and thicken the gravy – about another half hour. Cool.
▶ Preheat oven to 210°C (425°F). Roll out the pastry to line a medium-sized pie dish. Fill with the meat and gravy mixture. Cover with more pastry pricked with a few holes to let steam out. Bake in oven for 30 minutes, or until well browned. Serve with mashed or new potatoes and fresh peas.

Rhubarb Crumble

Serves 4

About 8 stalks rhubarb
100–200 g (3½–7 oz) sugar

CRUMBLE TOPPING
2 tablespoons each brown sugar, coconut, self-raising flour, soft butter

▶ Wash and chop rhubarb and cook with a liberal amount of sugar, to taste, until soft. Put into a tart dish. For topping, rub all ingredients together. Cover the rhubarb with this mixture and bake in a moderate oven (180°C, 350°F) until brown. Serve hot with cream.

Variations Try cooked apple with sultanas or strawberries; cooked pear with rhubarb; or stewed peaches.

Chips

potatoes (I use pontiacs or desirees)
extra-virgin olive oil

▶ Peel, wash and slice your potatoes into chips and boil in water until cooked but not too soft. Drain well. Heat the oil until it smokes, add the chips and do not disturb until they have formed a crust – otherwise they will break up. Cook until golden brown, drain well, pat with absorbent paper and serve immediately.

Trifle

200 g (7 oz) sugar
3 punnets (750 g/1½ lb) strawberries
3 punnets (750 g/1½ lb) raspberries
½ quantity crème anglaise (see recipe page 147)
one layer of sponge cake (see recipe page 128)
1 strawberry or raspberry jelly sachet, made up to 500 ml (scant pint) jelly
300 ml (10 fl oz) cream, whipped
flaked almonds, toasted

► Slice most of the strawberries (but keep some nice ones aside, whole, for decoration), combine with half the sugar and leave to stand at room temperature for a couple of hours. Put the raspberries and the remaining sugar into a saucepan, heat through, then sieve out the seeds.

► To assemble, put layers of raspberry sauce, crème anglaise, cake (sliced horizontally in half so it makes two layers) and cold, chopped jelly into a bowl. Spread whipped cream over the top, then pipe rosettes of cream and top with whole strawberries. Sprinkle toasted flaked almonds all over.

August

THE FIRST foal of the season is born. She surprised us all and was probably five hours old before we found her. Now everyone is on foal alert and in front of the manager's house at night lights are turned on to the mares who are closest to foaling. These lights are kept on till very late and after that an intercom-alarm worn by the mare sounds whenever she lies down. Being present at a birth is a moving experience, under the night sky, with everything still, and a mother in labour, trusting us to help her.

The wind is driving me crazy, the constant buffeting, the noise, the inescapability. It doesn't soothe like rain. It pounds and seems to get right inside one's head, flattening all our moods to utter gloom. Yet there can be no slowing down. The garden does not permit time off.

The Cottage Garden is at last nicely organised, all mulched, fed, tidied and planted, but down in the border beds the poppies need thinning and the Walled Garden looks sadly neglected. There the pink pansies have been disappointing, the flowers look moth-eaten and a bit dreary – like I feel. I will have to think of something pretty and fast-growing to put with them. It's too early for cleome: the seeds are only now being raised in the nursery. Perhaps we could try some apricot

Facing page: Polly, Sascha and I in the Poplar Grove

nicotiana edged with blue lobelia. This garden is a late flowering one, so we'll mulch and feed it and plant next month.

I must not panic – not yet. The whole garden is not fit to be seen and it must be ready for visitors in only two months. I think the wind, among other things, blows away one's confidence.

At last we are re-designing the nursery so that propagation can be done more easily. We need more of everything: a larger igloo with benches at the right height for all our bad backs, more shadecloth area for hardening off our cuttings, more long trays for striking them in. The best so far have been some disused feeding troughs we found in the barn. Holes were drilled along the base, then they were filled with a layer of sand and a mixture of compost and potting mix.

Seed collecting is another important job that up until now has been more miss than hit. Seed catalogues are my fetish, as much as horse catalogues are Rob's, particularly ones that feature new and exotic varieties. Back in the garden there are a good many everyday plants that need to be allowed the untidy business of going to seed, their large heads collected, hung up, and when the seeds finally drop, put into paper bags and labelled.

My friend Margaret gave me some of her marigolds and a bag of dried heads so that I could collect the seed. The marigolds are a tall variety with rusty brown flowers, a similar shade to wallflowers. After lifting them somewhat roughly from her garden, dropping them on the way in the car as the old plastic pot disintegrated in my hands, then driving them for three hours to the farm and planting them out in horror winds and the worst frosts this winter, I fear they may not survive. They've been cut back, to give them the best chance, but I'm glad I've got the seeds, for this variety of marigold, unlike some of its more garish relatives, is well worth having.

Planting and more planting. Planting lobelia and apricot nicotiana in the Walled Garden, rudbeckias and strawflowers in the Bright Border, more bidens at the front steps and pretty pink snapdragons in pots. I've also potted up foxgloves and white violets for odd spots in the shade.

An icy wind blew throughout the day, making our eyes water and hair stand on end, an unrelenting battering which shredded good spirits.

This is another palm planting day. Six eight-metre-high cabbage palms arrived on the back of a truck early. An excavator dug holes and the tractor, with its front-end loader, moved soil for planting. This is not a job for me to get too close to once the planting sites are pegged. It's hard work planting fully grown trees. I have had most success with palms as their roots are shallow and matted in a large ball, which means they transplant very well as long as the planting is followed up with frequent good waterings.

The Canary Island palms at the front of the house look as though they have always been there. Three came from Sydney and another two from the Dungog RSL Club, removed in order to make way for wheelchair access to the club. Their removal caused a momentary stir among some locals and hit the front page of the free press news: 'Trees on the Move'. It was a shame for those who loved them where they were, but at least they have thrived in their new home and the bats just love the berries.

Nine degrees above average and the wisteria pods began exploding like pop guns. Tiny green shoots are appearing on the American ash. Spring is coming. A full moon, all pale and silvery, and a mopoke calling across the night.

I almost forgot to mention the two varieties of blue iris that flower for weeks on end at this time of year. The Argentinian one, with straight spiked leaves and pretty deep blue flowers, one per stem. The other, the *Iris japonica,* a softer powder blue, with flowers that have fringes like eye lashes. Both establish easily but like to be left alone.

It is the end of winter. White cockatoos look for oats in the horse paddocks. They cry like babies. Four king parrots swoop into the camphor laurel near the kitchen door to eat the berries, and down at the creek, a brilliant azure kingfisher darts back and forth into the water, after small fish. Splashes of colour everywhere in a khaki landscape.

The garden is beginning to puff up under the warmer sunshine. New shoots appear on the mop-top robinias and the may is coming into flower. I am worried about predictions of drought that we have almost regularly in the news now. A dry spring is depressing to farmers and gardeners alike. Already we are dragging irrigators about and shaking our heads at glorious blue skies. 'Lovely weather' they say in the city, but we want rain.

The death of my mother
2nd August

It is very difficult to sit here when every thought is focused on what is so painful to recall. I have been promising myself all week that I would do it, and now that the day is here I must try. Most of the time I am able to lock my thoughts of her away and not face up to the fact that I will never see her again. This was the day last year that my mother died.

The night before she died she said her last words to me, 'Turn me over', and I put my arms under her terribly thin body – not worried about diets and cholesterol now – trying not to hurt her. I felt utterly inept, and very clumsy, for I could not bear to touch the ugly lumps that had grown secretly deep inside her lungs and were now protruding from her back. Dying for her was a hideous business.

The months leading up to and following her death were the worst I have experienced. So hard to talk to her alone, for even a few minutes, and when I could, not saying what I really wanted to, 'God, I'll miss you'. Times alone, when it was just me and her, were always precious.

Now grief is overwhelmed by impotent anger. I knew better than to expect life to be fair, but I had always had a fancy that one day she would spread her wings and do all the things she longed for – to travel the world, visit galleries and gardens, and have fun.

I want to cry out 'Unfair'. Unfair to die before she had the chance. It might have all been different, but there's no point my having regrets, for each life is filled with choice and she chose her own path.

She was too good. Her spirit big and generous, her sweet nature cheerful and optimistic, her patience the stuff of legends. She taught me so many things in her own gentle way, especially to recognise the real worth in others and to shun snobbery, the false and self-important, and to recognise that even though life can be dreary and unfair, there is always something to be glad about.

She deserved so much and there was so much I wanted to give her. We used to build many a castle in the air – just her and me, over lunch, a few precious moments spent dreaming – and she would smile. I am from another generation and I can never know what it was to see the world through her eyes.

Now, as I sit here on a bench beside the water, I wish she could be here with me, watching the ducks. I long to hear her tell me about the shadows on the hill opposite and how they should be painted. I am sad when I think she can no longer see a day as beautiful as this one, feel the warm winter sun, the soft breeze, pick violets, walk along the creek at sunset with a beer in her hand.

Now there is only the soft clicking of a willy wagtail, a little way off, protecting her nest.

I have another thought that comforts me. For one who created so much happiness in the lives of others, she must have had a measure of contentment. In this garden, this place of fantasy that she inspired and helped me to create, slowly, very slowly, I accept that she is gone and I also accept the path in her life she chose – so different to my own.

> *But the effect of her being on those around her was incalculably diffusive:*
> *for the growing good of the world is partly dependent on unhistoric acts;*
> *and that things are not so ill with you and me as they might have been,*
> *is half owing to the number who lived faithfully a hidden life, and rest*
> *in unvisited tombs*

George Elliot *Middlemarch*

Many of the recipes my mother used were handed on to her by her mother, my grandmother. They were recipes devised in the Depression years, made of cheap ingredients and designed to fill a hungry family. A few I remember well, plain and practical, of another time and place, but part of my life.

Chocolate Cake

This cake is famous in our family as the one first taught to children. My daughter Rachel was three-years-old when my mother patiently watched her measure and stir the ingredients. At 27 she still knows the recipe by heart.

1 cup (200 g/7 oz) sugar
2 level tablespoons cocoa powder
1 cup (120 g/4 oz) self-raising flour, sifted
½ cup (125 ml/4 fl oz) milk
2 eggs
½ teaspoon vanilla essence
3 tablespoons margarine

► Place everything except margarine in a bowl. Melt margarine, pour over the ingredients in the bowl and beat really hard for 3 minutes. Bake in a moderate oven (180°C/350°F) for 20–25 minutes.

Teacake

This was an aunt's secret recipe. One day my mother watched her make it and took mental notes.

▶ Cream 1 tablespoon butter with ½ cup (200 g/7 oz) sugar. Add 1 egg, ½ cup (125 ml/4½ fl oz) of milk, 1 cup (120 g/4 oz) self-raising flour, sifted, and a pinch of salt. Bake in a well-greased and lined loaf tin in a moderate oven (180°C/350°F) for about 15 minutes.

Note The top of this cake often splits. For variety add a handful of currants. Serve straight from the oven, hot and buttered.

Curried Eggs

This was Mum's great standby for when there was no meat or much else with which to make a meal.

hardboiled eggs

SAUCE
½ teaspoon butter
1 tablespoon flour
250 ml (9 fl oz) milk
black pepper and salt
1 tablespoon curry powder (or to taste)
2 tablespoons chopped parsley or chives

▶ Make the sauce: melt the butter and cook the with the flour for a moment then add the milk gradually as it thickens. Season. Add herbs then eggs, in quarters.
▶ Mum used to serve this with rice or potatoes and other vegetables.

Green Tomato Pickles

There were always green tomatoes at the end of the season. This was one way of using them.

▶ Mix 1½ cups (300 g/11 oz) sugar, 1 tablespoon each cornflour, curry powder and salt with 1 cup (250 ml/9 fl oz) vinegar.
▶ Peel and chop 500 g (generous lb) green tomatoes, 500 g (generous lb) onions. Mix with other ingredients and cook for 15 minutes.

Hard Timers

We lived on these biscuits as children.

½ cup (125 ml/4 fl oz) dripping or butter
4 cups (500 g/generous lb) self-raising flour, sifted
2 cups (420 g/15 oz) sugar
2 beaten eggs
a sprinkle of nutmeg and a handful of currants

▶ Rub the shortening into the flour and sugar, add the currants and nutmeg, then mix to a dough with the eggs.
▶ Cut into rounds and bake at 200°C (400°F) for about 10 minutes.

Fig Jam

1.5 kg (3½ lb) figs
750 g (1½ lb) sugar
2 large lemons

▶ Peel figs, wash, then cut into quarters or smaller. Grate lemon rind finely over figs, add the sugar and lemon juice and leave to stand overnight.

▶ Next day, bring to the boil slowly and cook steadily until the jam jells.

Blackberry Shortbread

Growing up in the country in the fifties, in the days before blackberry bushes were considered a noxious weed, we had many happy outings picking berries by the bucketload.

about 2 punnets (500 g/1 lb) blackberries
75g (3 oz) butter
250 g (9 oz) plain flour
1 tablespoon baking powder
75g (3 oz) sugar
1 egg
2 tablespoons milk
extra sugar

▶ Rub the butter into the flour and baking powder, add sugar and form into a stiff dough with beaten egg and milk.
▶ Roll out and put a layer of pastry in a pie plate, cover well with the berries, sprinkle with some extra sugar and cover with remaining pastry.
▶ Bake for half an hour in a moderate oven (180°C/350°F).
▶ Serve hot or cold with cream.

September

SPRING is here and a flush of chrome-green spreads among the willows in the creek. I've been watching families of ducks on the dam and ducklings disappearing one by one. The eels are eating them. I will have to get the eel man back to set traps again; then, instead of eating ducklings, the eels can be exported somewhere and turned into pâté.

Buds are opening on the Powton tree, the wisteria and the white rose 'Seneca Alba', which is sometimes called the Cherokee rose. It is wild and very hardy, smothered in thorns on long canes and with the purest single flowers and golden stamens. I have planted several over old fences, in out-of-the-way places where they get little or no attention, and they positively flourish. Every spring masses of white flowers brighten up a corner somewhere in the distance.

As the days warm up jumpers are thrown aside and we garden in T-shirts, planting and composting relentlessly. White cosmos, rudbeckias, lobelia, and white and yellow marguerite daisies fill odd places among the foxgloves. Frost-blackened heliotropes are cut back and more white-flowering lamiums planted along shady edges. Under the Canary palms the helleborus flowers are a picture.

There is a faint hum in the garden – bees in the ranunculus. Some of the pink ranunculus look like peonies, other smaller ones like roses. I tried to photograph a bee inside one of the large cream flowers, but he rolled about so unexpectedly, scraping his legs, head over heels, and then my hand shook the camera.

It is Sunday and we ate lunch beside the dam today, watching the dwindling ducklings sail up and down, and I thought about Virginia Woolf filling her pockets with stones and walking into the water. Sometimes on days as perfect as this the unbearability of it all becomes more real.

It has suddenly turned wintry again, gusts of wind blowing blossoms every way, just when the Powton tree was starting to catch everyone's attention, its soft mauve, bell-shaped flowers looking somewhat like foxgloves.

I'm bent double over a fire and refusing to leave the house. Annie has given me the name of a good chimney sweep to call in when spring decides to stay. She gave me his name after her own chimney caught fire, and she endured the embarrassment of three fire engines arriving, sirens blaring, and a lady fire chief who admonished her lack of chimney maintenance. Annie lit the fire as she always did but this time as the flames rose up she threw a takeaway pizza carton on top, causing the flames to shoot up even higher and setting the entire chimney alight. Sparks threatened to enter the ceiling and put my friend's entire home at risk. She laughed about it afterwards, saying that it emphasised yet again the hidden dangers of takeaway food.

Glorious hedges of photinia and may – which appear like drifts of snow – in full flower. Later in summer it will be the turn of the plumbagos and oleanders. These living boundaries create windbreaks and sheltered havens for countless small birds. The Spartans make the tallest walls. They are fast-growing, too, nearly three metres high after only two years. Murrayas are a good, solid, dark-green backdrop with highly perfumed summer flowers. Where needed clipped box, both English and Japanese, give definition to the outline of garden beds.

We are planting shades of lemon and blue Louisiana iris along the north bank of the dam. Cow manure has been collected from the paddocks especially for this purpose. Down on bended knees again, planting, as if praying.

Facing page, clockwise from top left: The French Lady standing among the blossoms; The Powton tree; Ranunculus; Wisteria growing on the terrace overlooking the Walled Garden

This is the beginning of spring, the time of year when gardeners begin to open their gates to visitors. For a short while we are able to enjoy the early spring blooms, particularly the wisterias, and it is a wonderful way to spend a few hours or even a whole day, wandering around other people's gardens with the chance of picking up a new idea or two. I enjoy looking at how other people solve their gardening problems, and seeing the sort of plants that do well in our region.

This particular weekend there were a number of gardens to choose from as both the Australian Open Garden Scheme and the Maitland Garden Ramble had gardens on show. So Rob and I got out the maps and set off eager to visit four gardens in the district.

At the end of the main street in Dungog we stopped for lunch, then proceeded to the first garden. 'Can you guess the sex of this gardener?' I asked at the first stop. 'A man, of course.' If the bush rock beds filled with native plants had not given the game away – for a lot of men I know seem to love them – then the nude with its legs in the air, plonked in a bird bath, did. A pair of entwined naked lovers under a grevillea clinched it. Women of a more delicate nature – not like me – float flowers in bird baths instead, and their ornaments with bosoms usually wear drapes.

I am as much interested in the gardener as in the garden, for herein lies a tale. What are they like, this man in the Akubra hat enthusiastically towing a group of visitors to view his latest bush rock beds, or the flower-floating lady in her dainty silk blouse? It was so nice to see them out and about, so obviously pleased to see us, and proud of their gardens. But of the four gardens visited two were without human contact. Either hiding inside or out for the day, I supposed, bored or frightened, unable to face our intrusion into their private worlds.

It is this private world that is so fascinating. What are you like underneath those gardening gloves and straw hats? What thoughts fill your minds? Are they of life and love or compost and weeds? I always think that to be a gardener one must at heart be romantic, but I'm inclined to doubt this of certain sorts of men in khaki overalls, and sensible boots and hats.

The blue wisterias fill the air with perfume. The pink and whites are slower to open. Crabapples, photinias, pears, peaches and plums are suddenly in bloom. Five flowers appeared on the pink clematis over the arbour this morning.

I have been reminding myself of Schubert, and 'The Trout' is rippling about the house. I used to sing 'The Linden Tree' many years ago. Schubert, shy, sick, lonely, dead at thirty-four, who inspired me to study music. Nightly practice nearly drove my sister and two brothers mad in the tiny two-and-a-half bedroom cottage we called home. Thumps on the wall, a long time ago, and me practising arpeggios and singing 'The Linden Tree' and driving them mad. Sometimes the music is so beautiful it is painful to hear. It is also painful to remember and it is better to go for a quiet walk along the creek and listen to the birds.

At last I am alone for the day and slowly able to sink into myself and think for a while. That is, instead of incessantly feeding people, making things orderly and comfortable. The domestic life weighs upon the creative one, all but grinding it into nothingness.

Much longed for spring rains came this week. In the face of dire drought warnings, rain swept across the state, and outside the frog chorus is in full swing. I feel truly happy. One of those country fellows who think they know everything once told me I would never have a garden here, and I'm smiling and thinking, so far so good.

More Lousiana iris have arrived, courtesy of Heather the iris lady from Turramurra. Another two hundred. This garden swallows plants by the hundreds and thousands and they are scarcely noticed. I have chosen unnamed varieties that are much cheaper than the named, and I think just as lovely. Cut, I am told, they will last in a vase for two weeks, and to prove the point Heather brought two flowering stems, each at least a metre in length, for me to enjoy inside. She has also brought the variegated version of the Iris japonica that I love so much.

The rain continues, which is absolutely fabulous four weeks before our first open days. James and David are weeding rose gardens and planting Korean box hedges around them. These box hedges look like the Japanese in leaf form, but do not grow as high. They make an excellent little border plant and have a much softer look. Amanda, covered in mud from head to foot, is planting iris at the dam edge.

Gardening

To work in a garden is one of life's great pleasures, but it is also hard work. I could never have a garden like this unless I was out in it often, in the oldest of clothes, covered in dirt, and at day's end aching in every joint and muscle.

That is the first important requirement, physical labour. Gardens do not happen by dreaming about them.

After that comes the soil. Gardeners think constantly about soil and also work constantly at improving it. People sometimes say to me, 'You must have good soil here,' but the opposite is true. Heavy clay topped with a scrape of topsoil has meant constant building up and feeding. Each year we barrow onto the garden beds 1000 kg of Dynamic Lifter, 500 kg of blood and bone, 40 cubic metres of mushroom compost, 500 kg of cow manure, old urine-drenched and manure-rich straw from the stables, lucerne straw in spring, and liquid fertilisers from the commercially prepared to the simplest mixture of dung and water carried about in garbage bins.

When the soil is just right a fork or spade will go in easily all the way. It will be crumbly, full of dark humus and worms. None of this is God-given. It is worked for and is neverending.

The other essential is water. Plants, like people, need food and water and wishing for rain is simply not good enough. If the soil dries out it will turn to dust and nothing will grow.

After this, if the plants are to have the best chance, the soil should be as free from roots and weeds as possible, and then when they do very well, as they no doubt must, there is all the cutting back and trimming to be done.

Seafood Chowder

This hearty soup is one I make a lot, because it is so useful for when it comes to feeding a large group of people. On the occasion that a film crew came to Torryburn, combined with gardeners and assorted others, this is what we had. It is nothing more than a hot Vichyssoise with seafood added at the end, but it is very good. The recipe serves 6, but can be doubled or tripled, as required.

2 leeks, peeled, washed and chopped
1 large onion, peeled, washed and chopped
knob of butter
black pepper, salt to taste
4 large potatoes, peeled, washed and chopped
milk
300 ml (10 fl oz) cream
2 x 425 g (15 oz) cans corn kernels
100 g (3½ oz) grated gruyère
5 tablespoons finely chopped parsley

SEAFOOD
choose any that you like: diced fish, green prawns, scallops, clams, shelled crab. For example, 500 g (generous lb) diced salmon, 12 green prawns, 12 scallops.

▶ Cook the leek and onion in the butter, add the potato, pepper and salt, cover with water and simmer until everything is soft.
▶ Purée in a blender. Thin with a little milk and finish with the cream. Stir in the corn, gruyère, parsley and seafood, until everything is cooked through. Adjust the seasoning.

Crab and Coconut Soup

Another seafood soup to make when fresh crab is readily available, already shelled and packed at the fish market.

2 tablespoons virgin olive oil
1 clove garlic, finely chopped
1 Spanish onion, finely chopped
1 piece ginger, peeled and chopped
handful each of parsley, chives and coriander, finely chopped
2 x 425 g (15 oz) cans tomatoes
2 x 400 ml (14 fl oz) cans coconut cream
2½ cups (1 pint) pure water
1 kg (2 lb) shelled crab
salt

▶ Heat the oil in a large pot, add the garlic, onion, ginger and herbs and gently fry till soft. Add the remaining ingredients except salt and simmer together for an hour. Add salt to taste.

October

THE GARDEN is at its prettiest in October and that is why I like to open it at this time to visitors. It is the middle of spring, the time when the garden seems to rise like the tide overnight.

The pink evening primrose that has flattened itself to the earth all through the winter is now standing on tiptoe. The tall yellow variety is up on stilts. Euphorbias with their soft green heads spring up everywhere as if to say, I bet you forgot about me. There are salvias of every hue, Queen Anne's lace, valerian, echiums with sensational large blue heads, old-fashioned watsonias – both pink and white – daisies, verbena, wallflowers, cornflowers, larkspurs, delphiniums, opium and tulip poppies, aquilegias and scabiosa. These are some of the flowers in the cottage beds.

GARDEN VISITORS

For the most part visitors to the garden are courteous and complimentary, not given to complaint and sensitive enough to step over and around plants that spill onto pathways. I am always amazed at how undisturbed things are after a weekend of hundreds of meandering pairs of feet.

The weeks leading up to an open weekend are particularly busy. Despite months of planning, there suddenly seem to be lots of empty spaces where nothing seems to be happening and a mountain of things to attend to at the last minute, to ensure that every single corner looks right. The mowing is endless, edging, trimming, weeding and then on the morning of the opening a final inspection with eagle eyes, pulling out yet another thistle as the first car drives through the gate.

For the two days before we open I cook sponge cakes – as many as I can, about twenty, to sell in slices with cups of tea. The sponge cake has become something of a tradition, not easily given up. When iced with passionfruit it is called 'Fly cake'!

Everyone on the farm, my brothers and sister and their families, help out on open days. Others come along as well, sometimes volunteers from the bushfire brigade or parents from the school, all willing to give time to raising funds for a community project of one kind or another. Someone sits at the entrance table under an umbrella collecting the money and getting the visitors' book signed, another parks cars. The tea and coffee table needs constant attention – urns topping up, milk jugs and sugar bowls refilling, sponge cakes to be iced and filled and cut – and then there is all the talking to be done.

By the end of the day we are exhausted. By the end of the second day we are ready to unwind in style, pour drinks, jump in the pool, shout hooray and generally let our hair down. But you can get caught! The last time we thought it was finally safe to relax, a volley of four-letter words filled the air and we were amazed to discover a very disgruntled latecomer kicking his car and fuming over a broken muffler. We managed to calm him down, tie his muffler back on, explain that the day was indeed over but he and his wife were most welcome to walk around anyway. I could hear him in the distance commenting with interest on the flowers in the vegetable garden and it was a relief when we saw our very last visitor go home happy that day.

While I love to show the flowers to others it's impossible to be absolutely satisfied. Either the poppies have finished a week too soon and have to be pulled out, or the sweetpeas are completely done, or the rain has spoiled the roses, or something else is not quite open. I'm also too aware of the garden's inadequacies, its youth, the fact that so many trees are still so tiny, pergolas not quite covered with roses, hoops that it will take two more seasons to fully entwine. There are areas that I've not gotten into yet and only have dreams for. Sometimes I can't even see the garden as it is, only as it might be one day.

Once I remember talking about a border of lavenders, waving my arms about and pointing into the distance. It was only when I saw the bewildered expression on my listener's face that I realised I was describing something that existed only in my mind's eye. There are times I have to pull myself up with a jolt and enjoy what is, what has been achieved thus far.

Facing page: The Bright Border

The Adamstown–Kotara Garden Club are my first visitors for the season, traipsing about in the wet, all rugged up, with umbrellas and sensible shoes. Gardeners never complain about rain and, despite doing more talking than I'm used to and needing to lie down afterwards to recover, it makes me very happy showing people the flowers, the walks, the arbours, sharing longings for beauty and a cup of tea on the verandah.

Other garden clubs came in coaches, always more women than men, some wearing embroidered name tags. Molong District Club were a particularly friendly group but unbeknown to them they brought strange troubled memories for me. As a little girl growing up in that town with its blue–green hills and tall golden poplars along the creek, I had felt a sense of my place in the world and it was a humble one – all home-made clothes.

The property owners, the graziers, were at the top of the ladder followed by the professional people. While respected, we were poor. The teachers loved my mother who made costumes for school plays, knitted gloves for the nuns and the priests – even though we were Methodists – and fed hungry neighbours' children after school on fried scones with golden syrup.

I think it was in kindergarten, sitting on the mat with the others of equal or even worse poverty – holes in jumpers, all knobbly knees and unkempt hair – while others were brushed and shiny in bought clothes, that I made up my mind to be the very best that I could be and one day show them all.

Now, as the Garden Club wandered about, I felt that the child on the mat had not changed at all. I still felt a tingle at being asked which street I had lived in and what was my grandmother's name. Perhaps one day I will return to Molong and lay that particular ghost to rest for good.

My next visitors were group from Sydney who were weekending in the Hunter and begged to call by. They didn't want coffee – but a bunch of parsley would be nice and they left a generous donation for the local school library.

Never have the roses been more glorious. I wander about in amazement at the strength and size of the bushes and flowers as big as plates. I am also convinced that putting 'Abraham Darby' in the Yellow Rose Garden was a mistake. Amanda says it has a yellow tinge, but to my eye it is pink.

'Titian' climbing on the red bricks of the house receives most attention, and 'Crépuscule' scrambling up a hoopway with the white clematis Montana headed in the opposite direction. What I thought was a climbing 'Iceberg' turns out to be 'Lamarque', so vigorous and pretty. In the Walled Garden, 'Mme Grégoire Staechelin' is splendid alongside deep purple salvias. And there are spires everywhere: delphiniums, foxgloves, larkspurs, and later there will be the acanthus, verbascums and hollyhocks. Tall flowering spires giving perpendicular strength to a canvas full of curves.

I am recovering from the first of our open weekends. In the aftermath of a big event like this I feel flattened. This time sad too, finding loved garden objects deliberately broken and thrown away. Who can say why even a child would do this?

There were exasperating moments dealing patiently with a gentleman who insists that I tell whoever is in charge – obviously not me – that the place needs a flagpole, a funny moment watching an old lady using her walking stick to point out to a group of bystanders a very large and healthy thistle among the poppies in the border, aggravating moments chastising bored children caught throwing gravel at each other and another attempting to let the pig out of her pen.

Yet I had stood at the end of the Bright Border filled with red poppies, pink poppies, yellow iris and orange geums and expectantly watched people's faces as they turned the corner and saw it for the first time. Red poppies! Red poppies and looks of delight. One elderly gentleman began to talk to me of the war, our lost men, the fields of Flanders, and tears shone in his eyes. Other old men sat in the Walled Garden shaking their heads, planning how they would alter their own gardens when they went home. A mixture of joy and disappointment and humanity with all its faults and goodness had passed through the garden that weekend.

October is the month of flowers. It is the moment of climax in a drama dictated by the seasons. It is a month full of exclamations and surprise, as if we feared for one moment nature might forget what it had to do.

My mother was born in October. This year she would have been seventy. Soon the hot winds will blow the poppies away and it will be time for another change.

Sponge Cake

6 eggs
150 g (5 oz) castor sugar
1 teaspoon vanilla essence
125 g (4 oz) self-raising flour

▶ Preheat the oven to 190°C (375°F).
▶ Separate the eggs. Beat the yolks with half the sugar until pale and very thick. Beat in the vanilla essence. Beat the whites with the remaining sugar until stiff. Spoon the whites on top of the yolk mixture. Sift the flour on top of that and fold everything together quickly and lightly. Pour the mixture into two greased and floured tins, the bases lined with the baking paper, and bake for about 20 minutes.
▶ When done, the cake should shrink from the edges and spring back when touched in the centre.
▶ When the cakes are cool, wrap in cling wrap until needed. Just before serving fill with fresh whipped cream, and ice (see below).

Variation For Chocolate Sponge, use 100 g (3½ oz) self-raising flour combined with 25 g (1 oz) cocoa powder.

Icings *Passionfruit:* 150 g (5 oz) icing sugar, 50 g (2 oz) soft butter and enough passionfruit pulp to make spreading consistency. *Chocolate:* 150 g (5 oz) icing sugar, 50 g (2 oz) butter, 1 tablespoon cocoa powder and milk to stir.

For a large serving

4 × 425 g (15 oz) cans diced tomatoes
1 bunch fresh basil, finely sliced
400 g (14 oz) ham, finely sliced
   (or substitute 500 g/generous lb mushrooms for vegetarian version)
6 tablespoons finely sliced spring onions
1 eggplant, sliced and baked in an oiled pan until soft
lasagne sheets, poached until soft and drained
grated cheese

CHEESE SAUCE
100 g (3½ oz) butter
100 g (3½ oz) plain flour
1 teaspoon salt
1 teaspoon pepper
750 ml (1¼ pints) milk
300 g (11 oz) grated gruyère

▶ Put tomatoes and basil together in a pan and simmer until thick. Fry ham and spring onions together until soft.
▶ Make a roux with butter, flour, pepper and salt, gradually whisk in the milk to thicken and stir in the gruyère at the end.
▶ Preheat the oven to 180°C (350°F). Assemble the lasagne in a large rectangular oven dish. Butter the dish. Put the some cheese sauce on the bottom, then pasta, then tomato sauce, eggplant, ham, pasta, cheese sauce, eggplant, tomato sauce, pasta and finally sprinkle some extra grated cheese on top. Bake in oven for about 30 minutes.

October

Goat's Cheese, Herb and Onion Tart

4 brown onions, sliced
knob of butter
2 teaspoons sugar
1 quantity plain pastry (see opposite)
1 cup mixed chopped herbs e.g. thyme, parsley, chives, oregano
200 g (7 oz) goat's cheese, crumbled
150 g (5 oz) grated gruyère
4 eggs
300 ml (10 fl oz) cream
300 ml (10 fl oz) milk
1 teaspoon salt
1 teaspoon pepper

▶ Cook onions in butter with sugar, until very soft.
▶ Line a quiche dish about 30 cm (12 in) across with pastry. Chill. Put the cooked onion all over the bottom, sprinkle over the herbs, then the goat's cheese, then the gruyère, then pour over the eggs beaten together with the milk, cream and pepper and salt.
▶ Bake at 180°C (350°F) for approximately 1 hour or until done.

Plain Pastry

275 g (10 oz) plain flour
pinch of salt
125 g (4 oz) unsalted butter
1 egg, beaten
50 ml (2 fl oz) cold water

BY MACHINE

Sift the flour and salt into the bowl. Put in the butter in small pieces and combine until the mixture resembles breadcrumbs. Work in the egg and water, a little at a time, until the mixture becomes a smooth ball. Chill for half an hour before rolling.

BY HAND

Sift the flour and salt into a bowl. Put in the butter in small pieces using your hands and combine until the mixture resembles breadcrumbs. Work in the egg and water, bit by bit, until the mixture is nice and smooth. Chill for half an hour before rolling.

½ quantity puff pastry (see recipe page 66)
6 large red (Spanish) onions
large knob of butter
2 tablespoons castor sugar
400 g (14 oz) fetta cheese
ground black pepper
150 ml (5 fl oz) cream

▶ Line a 25-cm (10-in) flan dish with puff pastry.
▶ Stew the peeled sliced onions slowly in the butter and sugar until very soft and golden brown. Put the onion into the pastry base. Dice and purée the fetta with the cream then smooth this over the onion like a lid. Bake at 180°C (350°F) for about an hour, or till done. Serve cold with dressed rocket leaves on top.

You can make individual tartlets and serve hot. The reason I serve the large one cold is that it makes it so much easier to cut.

Sponge Cake (see recipe page 128)

November

'ALBERTINE' is suddenly in flower, a blanket of pink moths. Two weeks later they are gone, then the garden turns blue. Jacarandas, bog sage, duranta, salvia, buddleia, hydrangeas, catmint, lavender and agapanthus fill the late spring garden.

It is very dry and we are constantly on the move with sprinklers. The grass browns and crunches underfoot and it is tough for the new tree plantings in the front park, which are beginning to die. Even the oleanders look hot and tired, dropping yellow leaves while searing winds and temperatures near 40°C scorch and batter everything. Now we are pulling things out, masses of shrivelled-up nasturtiums, and piling lucerne under roses.

The final garden opening is in late November and this time more than 900 people came. It was so hot I feared old ladies fainting. Every shady garden seat was filled, cold drinks flowed and, to my surprise, the sponge cakes completely eaten, yet again.

The curtain has finally come down and we can relax at last, forget about struggling to keep annuals alive, well past their prime. All the poppies had to come out, there was no doubt about it, and baby zinnias planted in their place. No one seemed to mind that the Bright Border was not very bright, at least the hollyhocks were splendid and one visitor felt positively cheered to see the garden stressed and brown as it made her feel better about her own.

Some people ask me if I actually work in the garden. Perhaps they imagine I am carried about on a litter. Sometimes I would like to be! How nice to lie in the shade and be plied with cold drinks and dainty sandwiches, instead of manuring all day in the heat. Now I would rather think about anything except gardens.

Dogs

Dogs, like children, need affection, discipline, companionship, things to look forward to, routine and truthfulness. They are great observers of human behaviour and can tell by your shoes what will happen next.

They have a wonderful communication system all their own, and they have also been clever enough to work out some of ours. They understand language, words and simple phrases such as 'Would you like a bone?' 'How about a walk?' 'Where are those naughty bunny wabbits?' Language relating to their experience, repeated clearly and often, is soon understood.

They like to be told they're good, given hugs and tickles under the armpits. Outings are essential, city walks on leads to smell the smells, wild country romps chasing bunny wabbits and trips in cars.

Unless they have been reared with children they don't like them. It's not just because children are short and lacking an air of authority, they squeal in high-pitched voices, shriek and cry, make sudden jerky movements, lurchings and staggerings, all unpredictable and irrational. Not at all as human beings generally behave.

Let a dog sleep nearby at night and the bonding will be complete, you will have a guardian with an eye upon you forever. The very first time that I let the puppies into my room, those yelping, furniture-chewing, piddling, scratching monsters settled down instantly, quiet as mice, barely daring to breathe for the next eight hours.

Max, my German Shepherd, lost one eye out of pure devotion and what he saw as his neverending duty, watching me, ever only a few paces behind, when carelessly I mowed some rocky ground. He used to take the lead in his mouth when we started out on walks as if he was leading me and not the other way round. One day he looked a bit listless, not quite himself. He took the lead in his mouth as he always did, looked at me with his sorrowful one eye and went off quietly with the vet. 'I'll be back,' I said, as I always do when leaving dogs behind, and I meant it. But I still feel a pang, for Max trusted me. I was not to know they would find him full of cancer. The phone call came. Did I want him woken so that I could say goodbye – but that would have been too much for both of us and I agreed to immediate euthanasia. If our situations had been reversed I hope he would have done the same for me.

In my experience dogs are very little different to us. Some are nicer than others, some more willing to please, others are pigheaded, selfish and greedy. Others are patient to a fault. They are all unique characters. They have the same physical and emotional needs as us, and blossom given half a chance, some affection, consistency and purpose.

I know when I look into my Sascha's yellow, wolfish, green in the dark, malamute eyes and Polly's pig-headed, brown button, red in the dark, poodle eyes, that when I die I won't be going anywhere special that they can't go as well.

Do you think dogs will be in heaven?
I tell you, they will be there long before us.
Robert Louis Stevenson

Polly, Sascha and myself in the Cottage Garden

November

Welsh Rarebit Soufflé

It is Amanda's birthday this month, so instead of the usual sandwiches for lunch I made a soufflé with all the flavours of a Welsh rarebit and lots of fresh herbs as well. One soufflé is really not enough for more than three unless it is to be a starter to the main meal. For 4–6 people, I usually make two.

1 large tablespoon butter
2 tablespoons plain flour
black pepper
1 teaspoon salt
400 ml (14 fl oz) milk
2 tablespoons Dijon mustard
2 tablespoons horseradish cream
1 cup fresh finely chopped herbs (e.g. chives, parsley, thyme and oregano)
150 g (5 oz) grated gruyère
4 eggs, separated

▶ Preheat oven to 225°C (450°F).
▶ Melt the butter, stir in the flour and cook together for half a minute. Add pepper, salt and milk gradually, as it thickens, to make a white sauce. Stir in the mustard, horseradish, herbs and cheese.
▶ When smooth, remove from heat and stir in the egg yolks. Pour into a bowl to cool slightly.
▶ Whisk egg whites. Fold into mixture and pour into buttered soufflé dish. Bake for 30–35 minutes or until done (an inserted knife will come out clean). It is best that the oven is not fan-forced.
▶ Serve with a salad of rocket and toasted pinenuts.

Facing page: The Cottage Garden

An excellent soufflé that can be prepared well in advance and is an ideal starter or light lunch, accompanied by a leaf salad. This recipe makes 10 individual soufflés.

50 g (2 oz) butter
50 g (2 oz) plain flour
black pepper – a good grinding
large pinch salt
1 heaped tablespoon Dijon mustard
400 ml (14 fl oz) milk
150 g (5 oz) grated cheese
    (I use gruyère, cheddar or parmesan, or a mixture of all three)
4 eggs, separated
extra soft butter

SAUCE
600 ml (1 pint) cream
100 g (3½ oz) grated gruyère
black pepper to taste
salt to taste

▶ Melt the butter in a pan. Add flour, salt and pepper and cook for half a minute, then stir in the mustard. Add the milk gradually, stirring while it gradually thickens, then stir in the cheese and cook until smooth. Take the pan off the heat and stir in the 4 egg yolks. Put into a bowl and allow to cool.

▶ Preheat the oven to 225°C (430°F). Prepare the individual moulds. I use dariole moulds rather than the traditional soufflé variety. They hold approximately 125 ml (4 fl oz) liquid. These should be well buttered and a piece of buttered foil put into the base of each.

▶ Beat the egg whites to stiff peaks. Fold into the cheese sauce mixture and fill the moulds. Cook for 20 minutes or till done. Rest for 5 minutes, then unmould onto a plate. These will keep very well under clear plastic wrap in the refrigerator for several days.

▶ To serve, make sauce: put all the ingredients together in a pan and cook gently, stirring continuously until smooth and thickened. Warm through soufflés in a microwave or moderate oven, mask with the hot sauce and glaze under a very hot grill.

December

DECEMBER in the garden is a time of undoing what has been done.
Wheelbarrow loads of vegetation are pulled out and carted away and
manure-rich wood shavings from the stables spread liberally over the
bare places. This is the time of year we prepare yearlings for the
summer sales, and while they spend the days indoors, away from the
sun, there is a plentiful supply of stable mulch.

Everything is dead or shaggy, and I feel too listless to care or to
work either. There are many things I would rather do than battle flies
with perspiration dripping off end of my nose and startled all the
while by sudden movements, thinking it might be a snake. Yesterday a
young hare leapt out of the Herb Garden as I picked basil for dinner,
and an eagle landed on a fence, then flew off with a snake in its grip,
trailing behind, all limp like a liquorice strap.

The garden is falling apart, its wildness overwhelming, too hot to
work in, winds knocking us about. Smoke hangs over the hills like
ghastly rain clouds. Fires have reached the edge of the town and are
burning all the way to Allynbrook, stranding one old lady who is being
cared for by a family worried about their own land and fences. Gum
trees crackle, all brittle, shedding bark and branches. The whole world
feels set to explode and we long for rain.

But evening brings only thunder and lightning and when lightning
strikes a tree on the hill across the road, we call the Volunteer
Bushfire Brigade. The men inspect the flames and decide that there is
little to be done. The best thing to do is to go home and have some
Christmas cheer – a few beers.

CHRISTMAS

All this as Christmas approaches and the pressure mounts to be organised, all clean and tidied up, wrapped, well stocked and merry. Windows are washed, dusty yellow stalks that once were lawns are mown, and Eddie the electrician hangs fairy lights in the silky oak, turning it into a glowing pyramid.

Our farm Christmas party is held under the stars on a night fanned by a cool breeze. Dainty Amanda is Santa, plumped out with pillows, arriving on the ride-on-mower Santamobile, under an arc of coloured lights, emerging from the blackness, noisy and ludicrous.

The expectations of Christmas, the lists of people, presents, cards, food, are ticked off one by one, inbetween interminable shopping trips. There is a feeling that things and someone will be forgotten, duties miscarried, feelings hurt, not enough cream for the puddings.

Dickens' description of Dingley Dell is my particular Christmas fantasy. Everything jolly and snug, cherubic Mr Pickwick and motley friends Tupman, Winkle and Snodgrass, gift-of-the-gab Sam Weller, Mr Wardle and family, all gathered at Dingley Dell, with fires in the grate, hot punch, mistletoe, carol singing, steaming food, and everyone cosy and smiling and pleased to see the others.

But our Christmas is not like that, quite apart from the obvious Southern hemisphere differences – the scene is air-conditioned, the drinks are on ice and the pall of grey on the horizon is bushfire smoke, not snow clouds. It is a time of great expectations and sometimes these cannot be met. Not to everyone's satisfaction.

There are a great many tensions that spring up from differences within families, different personalities, different beliefs, values, different ideas about what constitutes the perfect Christmas time for them. Nostalgia also bubbles up at this time, with its longing to get the children together for just a few festive hours, everyone under one roof, just like it used to be. It does not seem a lot to ask and usually isn't, if there is understanding and goodwill on both sides.

But if the children are middle aged and their own children grown, they may well have reached the point of longing to spend Christmas in their own way, well away from family connections. Get-togethers that start to acquire the flavour of duty are no fun at all.

This should be a time to express love, not to fulfil obligations. Christmas will never be as it once was. Nothing stays the same and the magic of the past cannot be recalled. If possible we move on and create new, but different, magic.

My growing cynicism – almost to the 'bah humbug' stage – is softened on reflection of happy times, whipping soap flakes into fake snow, putting the most beautiful pearl-covered fairy on top of the tree, sixpences in puddings, a bag of mysterious bulges at the end of the bed.

It is probably time for me to take a step back and adopt a more relaxed approach to the frantic final flurry that Christmas has become.

I long for flexibility, spontaneity, and good humour. I long for a real sense of peace and goodwill. I long for understanding without resentment and real thoughtfulness. Above all I long for each and everyone I know, to respect each and every other, and feel happy that this time be spent where, with whom, and in whatever manner they please. Happy Christmas.

CHRISTMAS FOOD

We have a barbecue and accompanying dips at our farm Christmas party.

Barbecued Octopus and Salmon

2 kg (5 lb) baby octopus, heads cut off and thoroughly washed
1 salmon, filleted, skinned, deboned and cut into serving portions

OCTOPUS MARINADE
1 bunch basil, chopped
3 or 4 small chillies
black pepper to taste
2 cloves garlic, chopped
60 ml (3 fl oz) balsamic vinegar
extra-virgin olive oil, enough to make a marinade consistency

SALMON MARINADE
1 root ginger, grated
250 ml (9 fl oz) honey
500 ml (scant pint) soy sauce
2 cloves garlic, finely chopped
black pepper

▶ Put all octopus marinade ingredients into a blender to combine. Cover the octopus thoroughly with this mixture and leave for several hours before cooking.
▶ Combine all salmon marinade ingredients and coat the salmon portions thoroughly. Set aside for several hours before the barbecue.
▶ When barbecuing, make sure the seafood isn't overcooked.

Guacamole

3 nice big ripe avocados
1 tablespoon sweet chilli sauce (or to taste)
juice of 1 lemon
black pepper to taste
salt to taste
50 g (2 oz) grated parmesan
1 small Spanish onion, chopped finely

▶ Combine all the ingredients and serve with corn chips.

Crab Cakes with Dipping Sauces

Serves 6

500 g (generous lb) cooked, shelled crab meat
2 cloves garlic, finely chopped
3 spring onions, finely sliced
2 fresh chillies, finely chopped
2 tablespoons grated fresh ginger
1 bunch coriander, chopped
butter
2 tablespoons Thai fish sauce
1 egg
a mixture of fresh breadcrumbs and desiccated coconut

▶ Cook the garlic, spring onions, chillies, ginger and coriander in the butter so as to make everything soft. Mix with the crab, stir in the fish sauce and the egg. Roll the crab mixture into balls and dip into the breadcrumb mixture. Fry on both sides, put into a buttered oven dish and warm through. Serve with the accompanying sauces.

SAUCES
1. 125 ml (4 fl oz) sweet chilli sauce mixed with fresh lime juice to taste.
2. Fresh tomato purée with a sliced spring onion, a crushed garlic clove, a chopped chilli and 2 tablespoons finely chopped basil.

Little Christmas Puddings

This recipe was given to me by my good friend and colleague from You & Me days, Barbara Whitehouse. Makes 10 puddings.

A
225 g (8 oz) brown sugar
225 g (8 oz) unsalted butter
grated rind of 1 orange

B
4 eggs, beaten

C
225 g (8 oz) raisins, chopped
50 g (2 oz) mixed peel
225 g (8 oz) sultanas
100 g (3½ oz) currants
50 g (2 oz) glacé apricots or pineapple, chopped

D
150 g (5 oz) plain flour
½ teaspoon ground ginger
1 teaspoon mixed spice
½ teaspoon cinnamon

E
50 g (2 oz) almonds, chopped
50 g (2 oz) carrot, grated
100 g (3½ oz) soft white breadcrumbs
rum

10 x 150 ml (5 fl oz) pudding moulds

▶ Mix all the fruit listed under C together in a large bowl. Sprinkle liberally with rum and leave to soak overnight.

▶ Cream together the ingredients listed under A and add the beaten eggs. Sift all the dry ingredients listed under D together. Now add C, D and E gradually and alternately to the A and B mixture.

▶ Butter the moulds thoroughly and line the base of each with a circle of kitchen greaseproof or parchment paper. Spoon the mixture in and cover tightly with buttered aluminium foil. Cook in a baking pan filled with enough water to come half way up the sides of the moulds. Bake in a moderate 180°C (350°F) oven for 1½ hours. When done, the puddings will feel firm to touch and an inserted skewer will come out hot and clean.

▶ Serve with crème anglaise (see below).

Crème Anglaise

10 egg yolks
200 g (7 oz) castor sugar
900 ml (1½ pints) cream

▶ Whisk the egg yolks and sugar together until they are thick, pale and creamy.

▶ Scald the cream, then pour in a slow steady stream into the yolk/sugar mixture, while continuing to whisk slowly. When combined, put the mixture back into the saucepan and cook gently, stirring all the while, until the custard thickens to coat the back of your spoon. Take care not to let it boil. When cooked, pour through a sieve into a bowl and leave to cool.

Note For a rich vanilla sauce, the method of preparation is exactly the same, with the addition of 2 good vanilla beans. Split the beans lengthwise, scraping their powdery black centres into the cream 1 hour before proceeding with the recipe. Add the scraped pods as well to the cream to develop a fuller vanilla flavour. The beans will be removed when you strain the custard at the end. For a small quantity, this recipe can be halved.

4 punnets (1 kg/2 lb) raspberries
8 large slices white bread, crusts removed
300 g (11 oz) castor sugar

▶ Put three-quarters of the raspberries and half the sugar into a pan and heat through very well. Sieve to remove seeds and set aside as the sauce.
▶ Do the same with the remaining raspberries and sugar, but do not heat for quite as long, so that the berries hold their shape.
▶ Pour some of the sauce into a medium-sized bowl. Put one slice of bread into the bottom, then another four slices at the sides. Cut two slices into triangles to fill in the gaps. Put the just cooked raspberries into the centre of the bread, fold the bread over, put the remaining slice on top and cover very well with the rest of the sauce, allowing it to trickle down the sides and leave no white of the bread showing. Put into the refrigerator to set. Unmould and serve with cream.

NEW YEAR'S EVE

This is the last day of the year and we have not had rain, real rain, for three months.

I think a lot about the garden. Wonder about the sense of it all. It makes sense to the kookaburras, no doubt, always sitting still, watching. I wonder how long I can let the summer weeds take over, some more than a metre high with large seed heads.

Amanda left just before Christmas, not knowing if she would be able to return. Every Monday for three years she has been my gardening companion, doing all the things that I forget, watering thirsty pots, feeding them, trimming box hedges. She appears tireless but I know she is tired and at a turning point, looking for something else to do. I won't say to myself that I will miss her. I won't think about it just yet.

We spend the days dragging hoses about, watering trees that are probably already in the last stages of dying. It will rain one day. My diary is filled with this daily longing. It's nothing new. We have been through droughts before. It's just that the garden is so much bigger now, so much more vulnerable.

Night comes and I turn the fairy lights on in the silky oak, knowing that people passing along the road will see it. It looks grand and hopeful, a glowing sign of life struggling up out of the dark.

The garden sinks into the night and the white flowers are the last to fade from sight. Always plant white flowers for the night, someone once said.

So the year ends. The fairy lights sparkle, the dogs kill a rat, and I cook dinner as I have a thousand times before, and wonder what other people are doing.

As I go to bed I can see the lights of distant neighbours, their home lit up like a monastery on a hill, mainly men, I imagine, sitting around drinking beer and waiting for midnight.

The Southern Cross twinkles like more fairy lights in a cloudless sky. And the year ends.

Afterwards

THE NEW Year brought much that was longed for.

Rain fell in sheets, filling all the dams, flushing out stagnant ponds in the creek, and causing minor flooding throughout the Hunter Valley. Dorothea's film of green spread once more across the landscape, and struggling small trees sprouted tender shoots.

Hope returned. The garden would survive. A new circular bed for lavender was pegged out. I marched up and down making new plans and writing lists. More trees were ordered for the front park, more Louisiana iris planted at the dam, rose arbours erected and roses planted, mainly climbers and in particular favourites like 'Zéphirine Drouhin' and 'Titian'.

To our dismay James left, to pursue his own dreams and to catch up on work of his own. Nothing stays the same, and he left us shaking our heads and wondering how we would ever manage without him. Finding someone new meant sifting through those who 'hated oleanders', preferred 'native gardens', mowing to weeding, and those who were 'desperate for the work' but also wanted to 'choof off' every-so-often, for reasons indeterminate.

Amanda did not leave. She continues to be my supportive, optimistic, creative and funny gardening companion. We have that rare understanding which comes with seeing the world through similar eyes. Her connection with the garden deepens as it, and we, become stronger. Perhaps the garden is a reflection of ourselves.

This leads me to something important that I have not talked about. Torryburn is not my only home. I commute, and have been commuting backwards and forwards between city and country for these past ten years, living half my week here and half my week there, with all the complications that a split existence involves. Not only must there be two of everything, from toothbrushes to a desk at which to write, but there is a loss of centredness brought on by constant travelling, a sense of forgetting where one is, waking in the middle of the night and getting lost trying to find the bathroom.

When people visit me in the country and we walk about admiring the garden, they often say things like 'It must be hard to go back to the city. How can you bear to leave this?' Also, 'This is it. This is what life's about. You must be happy living here.' There is a good deal that is true in these sentiments, for the spirit is certainly nourished by connecting with the soil, the elements, the birds, the vast sky, these especially beautiful hills. We long for nature, to feel more closely the changing seasons, the natural passing of time. These are our animal instincts. Somehow we feel more in tune with ourselves once more. But the human side of us needs civilisation as well. There is a romantic city view of country life that fails to understand the profound isolation. This has nothing to do with solitude and the glorious peacefulness. This is the isolation of the mind, the lack of true connection with other people. The longing for real friendship and conversation passionate for ideas.

This is why it is necessary to return to the city. It is the other side to the coin of life, the need to share experience, the need to think and converse with interesting people from all walks of life, to go to concerts, the theatre, the opera, visit galleries, to absorb the wealth of artistic and intellectual expression that accumulates where people gather together and which is as necessary for a thirsty spirit as digging the soil in a peaceful place.

There is a dilemma in needing both elements in one's life, to 'have one's cake and eat it too', to live in two places for two very necessary but separate reasons. While some may reflect that this is indeed good fortune, there is a price to pay, however small. For me the price – apart from the exhaustion of driving up and down the freeway with painful sciatica, eating lollies to help keep awake, forever packing the car with groceries and dogs, the cat, the Esky and numerous other essentials, and then forgetting the toilet paper – is the sense of not being centred, of not being totally 'at home' when at home. Another price is constantly being interrupted in the garden, of being taken away from it and its daily needs. How much better things might be if I was able to spend a little of each day tending some small part in an ongoing fashion instead of constantly wrenching myself away from

Afterwards

tasks half done. This is the price I pay for living and also needing to live a complicated life. The yearning for simplicity can at times be overwhelming, but I know it can never be achieved – not for a very long time, perhaps not ever. For simplicity of this sort is denial of all the influences, all the bits and pieces that go to make up self.

We live in many worlds. Not just the worlds of city and country, but that wider one of the old world and the new. The soft European light and landscape blend deep inside us with the bright and wild Australian ones, both part of our complicated consciousness. Even our words reflect this mix, as meadows, streams and woods mix freely with paddocks, creeks and bush. To try to pare things down to a narrow parochial view is to destroy the rich complexity that makes us what we are.

I am wary of the sort of people who go about muttering about flagpoles, criticising the peacocks and fantail pigeons that trail about making their strange and wonderful sounds because they are not natives. I suppose the roses and daffodils are impure imports too, and the ornamental griffins and lions out of character in a landscape full of gum trees. Such people will never know what it is to hear, mingled, the plaintive peacock cry at dusk when at the same time the kookaburras swoop into the tallest gums and begin laughing like mad things. I don't want to have to choose between kookaburras and peacocks, lions and kangaroos. I want to be able to say, 'I'll have them all,' – for here they are inside, all part of me.

I know that I will never make another garden. Not somewhere else, not ever, not like this. Wherever I look it is green and bursting with life. The creek is flowing again, the roses the best they have ever been. Hollyhocks tower over our heads.

Torryburn, with all its setbacks and difficulties, without especially being planned, or reasoned, or thought out, or making much sense, has become a very special and beautiful place, and in my life and the lives of some others, an important one as well.

Appendices

ROSES

THE COTTAGE GARDEN AND SURROUNDS

'Aquarius'
'Avon'
'Brandy'
'Broadway'
'Chicago Peace'
'Crépuscule'
'Devon'
'Dorothy Perkins'
'Double Delight'
'Folklore'
'Golden Gloves'
'Graham Thomas'
'Granada'

'Guy Laroche'
'Iceberg'
'Kirsten'
'Maria Callas'
'Martin Frobisher'
'Moonbeam'
'Orana Gold'
'Papageno'
'Pascali'
'Peace'
'Princesse de Monaco'
'Pristine'
'Portrait'

'Regensberg'
Rosa eglanteria
'Sonia'
'Sutters Gold'
'Tamora'
'The Reeve'
'The Squire'
'Troilus'
'Valerie Swane'
'Voodoo'
'Wife of Bath'

THE BIG VEGETABLE GARDEN

'Abraham Darby'
'Alba Semi-plena'
'Amber Queen'
'Ballerina'
'Big Purple'
'Blanc Double de
   Coubert'
'Bolzanis'
'Buff Beauty'
'Camellia'
'Caprice'
'Céleste'
'Charmian'
'Chaucer'
'Cherry Vanilla'
'Chloris'
'Comtesse Riza du
   Parc'
'Cymbeline'
'Dapple Dawn'
'Duchesse de Brabant'
'Ferdinand Pichard'
'First Prize'

'Fragrant Plum'
'Frau Dagmar
   Hastrup'
'Frau Karl Druschki'
'Fritz Nobis'
'Frühlingsgold'
'Frühlingsmorgen'
'George Arends'
'Gina Lollobrigida'
'Grandpa Dickson'
'Grüss an Aachen'
'Hans Christian
   Andersen' (red)
'Iceberg'
'Ingrid Bergman'
'James Mitchell'
'Jaquenetta'
'Joyfulness'
'Just Joey'
'Lady Hillingdon'
'Lolita'
'Lordly Oberon'
'Madame Butterfly'

'Marigold'
Marjoram
'Max Graf'
'Mme Caroline
   Testout'
'Mme Legras de St
   Germain'
'Mme Plantier'
'Monsieur Tillier'
Moss Rose
'Moth'
'Mr Lincoln'
'Mrs B. R. Cant'
'Ophelia'
'Papa Meilland'
'Peace'
'Prosperity'
'Prospero'
'Queen Elizabeth'
Rosa devoniensis
Rosa officinalis syn. *R.
   gallica* var. *officinalis*
'Roseraie de l'Haÿ'

'Seduction'
'Silk Hat'
'Souvenir de la

Malmaison'
'Sparrieshoop'
'Spek's Yellow'

'Stanwell Perpetual'
'The Friar'
'Velvet Arrow'

ROADWAY BEDS

'Abraham Darby'
'Aotearoa'
'Arizona'
'Avon'
'Beautée'
'Canterbury'
'Charles Austin'
'Gertrude Jekyll'
'Happy Days'
'Heritage'
'Just Joey'
'Kardinal'

'Lordly Oberon'
'Lorraine Lee'
'Mary MacKillop'
'Mary Webb'
'Miriam'
'Oklahoma'
'Othello'
'Papa Meilland'
'Paradise'
'Peace'
'Perfect Moment'
'Precious Michelle'

'Sexy Rexy'
'Sheer Bliss'
'Sir Walter Raleigh'
'St Cecilia'
'Tamora'
'Voodoo'
'William
    Shakespeare'
'Woman's Day'
'Yellow Charles
    Austin'

CIRCULAR YELLOW ROSE GARDEN

'Abraham Darby'
'Buff Beauty'

'Gold Bunny'
'Golden Celebration'

'Graham Thomas'
'Yellow Charles Austin'

THE ROSE GARDEN

Red

'Australian
    Bicentennial Rose'
'Avon'
'Christian Dior'
'Dolly Parton'

'Gloire de Ducher'
'L.D. Braithwaite'
'Mme Isaac Pereire'
'Mr Lincoln'
'Papa Meilland'

'Red Coat'
'Scarlet Queen
    Elizabeth'
'The Dark Lady'
'Tuscany Superb'

Yellow and apricot

'Ambridge Rose'
'Apricot Delight'
'Brandy'
'Buff Beauty'

'Friesia'
'Golden Celebration'
'Helmut Schmidt'
'Lanvin'

'Leander'
'Midas Touch'
'Mrs Dudley Cross'
'Symphony'

Pink

'Bonica'
'Chaucer'
'Clair Matin'

'Mary Rose'
'Monsieur Tillier'
'Queen Elizabeth'

Rosa moyesii
'Geranium'

Overleaf: Looking across the dam and jetty to Torryburn

Plants grown at Torryburn

White

'Champagner'
'Frau Karl Druschki'
'Honor'

'Iceberg'
'Jardin de Bagatelle'
'J. F. Kennedy'

'Mme Hardy'
'Pascali'
'Virgo'

Mixed beds

'Aotearoa'
'Charles de Mills'
'Double Delight'
'Everest'
'Felicia'
'Gertrude Jekyll'

'Heritage'
'Honey Flow'
'Karen Blixen'
'Louise Odier'
'Mme Louis Lévêque'
'Mrs Fred Danks'

'Papa Meilland'
'Pinkie'
Rosa centifolia
'Sir Walter Raleigh'

Snake Gully rose beds

'Ambridge Rose'
'Belle Story'
'First Prize'
'Heritage'
'Jane Austen'

'Kathryn Morley'
'Mary Rose'
'Pascali'
'Peach Blossom'
'Perfume Delight'

'Pretty Jessica'
'Pristine'
'Sharifa Asma'
'Sonia'
'St Cecilia'

Climbers

'Albéric Barbier'
'Albertine'
'Blackboy'
'Blossomtime'
'Buff Beauty'
'Clair Matin'
'Constance Spry'
'Crépuscule'
'Golden Showers'
'Handel'

'Iceberg'
'Lamarque'
'Lorraine Lee'
'Mme Abel Chatenay'
'Mme Alfred
   Carrière'
'Mme Grégoire
   Staechelin'
'New Dawn'
'Pierre de Ronsard'

'Pinkie'
Rosa banksiae
Rosa devoniensis
'Seneca Alba'
'Thelma'
'Titian'
'Wedding Day'
'Zéphirine Drouhin'

PLANTS THAT FEATURE IN THE GARDEN
Small shrubs and cottage plants

Acanthus	*Acanthus* spp.
Agapanthus	*Agapanthus* spp.
Ageratum, perennial	*Ageratum houstonianum*
Alyssum, sweet	*Lobularia maritima*
Aquilegia, Columbine	*Aquilegia* spp.
Autumn crocus	*Crocus nudiflorus*
Bidens	*Bidens* spp.
Box, English, Japanese, Korean	*Buxus sempervirens* 'Suffruticosa', *B. microphylla* var. *microphylla, B. koreana*
Buddleia	*Buddleia davidii* 'Black Knight', 'Royal Red', 'Nanho Blue'
Calendula	*Calendula officinalis*
Catmint	*Nepeta* spp.
Clivia	*Clivia* sp.
Cornflower	*Centaurea cyanus*
Cosmos	*Cosmos* spp.
Daffodils and jonquils	*Narcissus* 'Erlicheer', *N.* 'Silver Chimes'
Delphinium	*Delphinium elatum* 'Pacific Giants', 'Blue Springs'
Duranta	*Duranta* spp.
Echium	*Echium* spp.
Evening primrose, yellow	*Oenothera odorata*
Forget-me-not	*Myosotis* spp.
Foxglove	*Digitalis* sp.
Gaillardia	*Gaillardia* spp.
Geum	*Geum* 'Mrs Bradshaw', *G.* 'Lady Stratheden'
Geraldton wax	*Chamelaucium uncinatum*
Heliotrope	*Heliotropum arborescens* 'Cherry Pie', *H.* 'Icecream'
Hellebore	*Helleborus* spp.
Hollyhock	*Alcea rosea*
Hosta	*Hosta* spp.
Hydrangea	*Hydrangea* spp.
Iris: Louisiana iris (water iris), Argentinian iris, Bearded iris, Japanese iris	*Iris* spp., *Iris japonica, I.* 'Venetian Waters'
Irish bells (Bells of Ireland)	*Moluccella laevis*
Lamium	*Lamium maculatum*
Larkspur	*Consolida* spp.

Plants grown at Torryburn

Lavender	*Lavandula angustifolia* 'Hidcote', *L. dentata, L. stoechas*
Lily, arum	*Zantedeschia aethiopica*
Lily, canna	*Canna* spp.
Lily, Gymea	*Doryanthes excelsa*
Loosestrife	*Lythrum* spp.
Love-in-a-mist	*Nigella damascena*
Marigold	*Tagetes* spp.
May bush	*Spiraea cantoniensis*
Nasturtium	*Tropaeolum major* 'Empress of India', 'Peach Melba', 'Alaska'
Oleander	*Nerium oleander*
Orange jessamine	*Murraya paniculata*
Pansy	*Viola* spp.
Penstemon	*Penstemon* spp.
Photinia	*Photinia glabra* 'Rubens'
Plectranthus	*Plectranthus* spp.
Plumbago	*Plumbago auriculata*
Poached-egg flower	*Limnanthes douglasii*
Poppy: Cottage poppy (inc. 'Rose Feathers', 'Swansdown White'), Flanders poppy, Iceland poppy, Oriental poppy, Tulip poppy	*Papaver nudicaule, P. orientale, P. rhoeas*
Poppy, Californian	*Romneya coulteri*
Queen Anne's lace	*Daucus carota*
Ranunculus	*Ranunculus* spp.
Rudbeckia	*Rudbeckia* spp.
Sages: Salvia, Bog sage	*Salvia argentia, S. azurea, S. leucantha, S. patens, S.* 'Black Knight', *S. uliginosa, S. 'Indigo Spires'*
Scabious	*Scabiosa* spp.
Seaside daisy	*Erigeron mucronatus* syn. *E. karvinskianus*
Sedum	*Sedum* 'Autumn Joy', *S. spectabile* 'Brilliant'
Snapdragon	*Antirrhinum majus*
Strawflower	*Helichrysum bracteatum*
Sunflower	*Helianthus* 'Lemon Queen'
Sweetpea	*Lathyrus odoratus*
Tagetes	*Tagetes* spp.
Tibouchina, Glory bush	*Tibouchina urvilleana* 'Alstonville'
Tobacco plant	*Nicotiana* spp.

Valerian	*Valeriana* spp.
Verbascum	*Verbascum* spp.
Verbena	*Verbena* spp.
Violet	*Viola* spp.
Wallflower	*Cheiranthus cheiri*
Windflower	*Anemone* x *hybrida*
Watsonia	*Watsonia* spp.
Zinnia	*Zinnia elegans*

Large shrubs and trees

Ash, American	*Fraxinus americana*
Crabapple	*Malus* spp.
Frangipani, native	*Hymenosporum flavum*
Jacaranda	*Jacaranda mimosifolia*
Juniper	*Juniperus chinensis* 'Spartan'
Lillypilly	*Acmena smithii*
Liquidambar	*Liquidambar styraciflua, L. formosana*
Mulberry, weeping	*Morus alba* 'Pendula'
Norfolk Island pine	*Araucaria heterophlla*
Oak, English	*Quercus robur*
Oak, Pin	*Quercus palustris*
Oak, Silky	*Grevillea robusta*
Palm, cabbage	*Livistonia* sp.
Palm, Canary Island	*Phoenix canariensis*
Persian silk tree	*Albizia julibrissin*
Poplar, Chinese	*Populus lasiocarpa*
Powton tree	*Paulownia* sp.
Peach, ornamental flowering	*Prunus persica*
Plum, ornamental flowering	*Prunus blireana*
Robinia, mop-top	*Robinia pseudacacia* 'Umbraculifera'
Tallow wood, Chinese Sapium	*sebiferum*
Wattle, Cootamundra	*Acacia baileyana*
Witch hazel, Persian	*Parrotia persica*

Climbing shrubs

Clematis	*Clemantis montana* var. 'Rubens', *C. montana* 'Tetrarose'
Potato vine	*Solanum jasminoides*
Snail creeper	*Phaseolus caracalla*
Wisteria	*Wisteria sinensis*

Vegetables

Arugula (roquette, rocket)

Beans, broad

Beans 'Purple King'

Beans, runner 'Scarlet Runner', 'Painted Lady'

Beetroot

Broccoli

Cabbage

Capsicum

Carrots

Cauliflower

Chicory (Italian radicchio)

Cucumber

Eggplant

Kale

Leek

Lettuce, oakleaf, Italian lollo, mesclun mix, cos, 'Rouge d'Hiver'

Mustard 'Red Giant'

Onions

Peas

Pumpkin

Radish

Rockmelon

Silverbeet 'Fordhook', 'Rainbow Mix'

Strawberry

Sweetcorn

Tomatoes 'Grosse Lisse', 'Mortgage Lifter', 'Tommy Toe', 'World's Largest Tomato'

Zucchini